TRAPPED in AMERICA'S SAFETY NET

CHICAGO STUDIES

IN AMERICAN POLITICS

A series edited by

BENJAMIN I. PAGE,

SUSAN HERBST,

LAWRENCE R. JACOBS,

and ADAM J. BERINSKY

TRAPPED in AMERICA'S SAFETY NET

One Family's Struggle

ANDREA LOUISE CAMPBELL

THE UNIVERSITY OF CHICAGO PRESS

Chicago and London

ANDREA LOUISE CAMPBELL is professor of political science at the
Massachusetts Institute of Technology. She is the author of *How Policies
Make Citizens* and coauthor of *The Delegated Welfare State*.

The University of Chicago Press, Chicago 60637
The University of Chicago Press, Ltd., London
© 2014 by The University of Chicago
All rights reserved. Published 2014.
Printed in the United States of America

23 22 21 20 19 18 17 16 15 14   1 2 3 4 5

ISBN-13: 978-0-226-14030-8 (cloth)
ISBN-13: 978-0-226-14044-5 (paper)
ISBN-13: 978-0-226-14058-2 (e-book)
DOI: 10.7208/chicago/9780226140582.001.0001

Library of Congress Cataloging-in-Publication Data

Campbell, Andrea Louis, 1966– author.
    Trapped in America's safety net : one family's struggle / Andrea Louise
    Campbell.
        pages cm — (Chicago studies in American politics)
        Includes bibliographical references and index.
        ISBN 978-0-226-14030-8 (hardcover : alkaline paper) — ISBN 978-0-226-14044-5
    (paperback : alkaline paper) — ISBN 978-0-226-14058-2 (e-book)   1. Public
    welfare—United States.   2. United States—Social policy—1993–   I. Title.
    II. Series: Chicago studies in American politics.
    HV91.C342 2014
    362.5'560973—dc23

                                                                    2014004817

♾ This paper meets the requirements of
ANSI/NISO Z39.48-1992 (Permanence of Paper).

For Logan

CONTENTS

PROLOGUE

On a crisp California morning in February 2012, my sister-in-law, Marcella Wagner, was driving down the interstate toward Chico State University, where she had just entered the nursing program. She was thinking about the day ahead when suddenly another driver swerved in front of her. To avoid a collision, she jerked the wheel hard, and her car veered off the freeway. It rolled over, crushing the roof. The other driver sped off, never to be found. Marcella was seven-and-a-half months pregnant. Miraculously, the baby survived and was not harmed. But Marcella was left a quadriplegic, paralyzed from the chest down and with little use of her hands. She will need a wheelchair and round-the-clock personal care assistance indefinitely.

The accident caused more than the physical and emotional devastation that upended Marcella's career plans. It also brought about an economic tragedy that hurtled her young family into the world of means-tested social assistance programs, the "safety net" of public programs for the poor. My brother, Dave Campbell, works for a small company that doesn't offer employee benefits. Nonetheless, before the accident Marcella had managed to secure health insurance for both her and the baby. Her pregnancy and sixty days' postpartum care was being covered by Access for Infants and Mothers (AIM), California's health insurance program for middle-income pregnant women. After the birth, Marcella would have been able to join the university's student health plan. The baby would be covered by the Children's Health Insurance Program (CHIP), the federal-state plan for lower-income children. Marcella and Dave thought they were all set. And then, with the accident, they fell down the social assistance rabbit hole.

Marcella had to enroll in Medicaid (Medi-Cal in California), the health insurance program for the poor, to cover her medical expenses. Even if she had had private health insurance, ultimately she would have needed to enroll in Medicaid: it's the only realistic source—public or private—for the long-term services she continues to need as a disabled person. Because Medicaid is a program for the poor, Marcella and Dave had to spend down their assets to qualify; they now live on a near-poverty income. And to stay eligible, they will have to remain under these strictures, perhaps for the rest of their lives.

As a social policy scholar, I thought I knew a lot about these programs. I had been teaching and writing about them for years, first at Harvard and then at MIT. Little did I anticipate how useless I would be to Dave and Marcella as they tried to navigate the extraordinarily complex American system of social assistance. And nothing prepared me for the Dickensian reality we encountered. I will never read the sober, measured manuals from government programs or the academic analyses of social policy in the same way again. Behind the statistics—and beyond the ideological battles over policy design—are human beings whose lives are molded, distorted, and stunted by policies purported to help them. I have come to wonder: if I as a social policy expert had little idea what these policies really do on the ground, how much do the politicians who created them know?

Not much, I suspect, and so the idea for this book was born. I first wrote about Dave and Marcella in a *New York Times* op-ed in April 2012, shortly after the Supreme Court heard oral arguments about the Affordable Care Act. I was deeply gratified when associate justice Ruth Bader Ginsburg cited my piece in her concurring opinion in *NFIB v. Sibelius*, upholding much of the ACA (although in the end the ACA doesn't help the permanently disabled much). And now I am fortunate to be able to tell Dave and Marcella's entire story.

The book begins by illustrating how common their situation is: their location on the income spectrum; the widespread lack of health insurance at their income, education, and age levels; the dearth of jobs with benefits in communities such as theirs; and the admissions, financial aid, and sheer capacity limits on education and training programs through which individuals might improve their situations. In chapter 2, Dave and Marcella learn the grim truth about how Medi-Cal works: the income test, the asset test, the other strictures. We all learn the dizzying complexity of the American safety net, with different programs run at different levels of government (county, state, federal), and with different eligibility criteria. And we learn of the limitations: the physicians who won't take Medi-Cal or CHIP; the prescriptions Marcella can't get filled because of Medi-Cal limits. Chapter 3 takes a step back, revealing how widespread the use of means-tested programs really is. It describes these programs targeted at the poor in relation to both universal social insurance programs and the private welfare system of employer-provided benefits, the "upper" tiers of social protections that Dave and Marcella had so desperately sought to enter before the accident. Chapter 4 shows how means-tested programs keep people poor, with low benefits, Draconian asset limits, and huge effective marginal tax rates that discourage working and trap recipients in poverty. Chapter 5 illustrates how widely social assistance varies across states, demonstrating how different Dave and Marcella's experience would have been if they happened to live elsewhere—which raises questions about the very nature of citizenship in the United States. Finally, chapter 6 explores whether Dave and Marcella can ever escape the Medicaid-induced restrictions under which they find themselves. Does the Obama administration's health reform—the Affordable Care Act—help? The short answer: no. Justice Ginsburg was right that the ACA helps many Americans in many ways, but not people like Marcella who need lifelong personal care assistance, for which Medicaid remains the sole source. The chapter also examines the characteristics of American social protections in cross-national comparison and discusses the future of social assistance in an era of fiscal constraint.

In the end, Dave and Marcella's story illustrates four main points about the nature of American social policy. First, our nation's social protections are divided into different tiers that provide vastly different experiences for recipients. Moreover, with demographic and economic change, the means-tested tier that many believe is residual is in fact becoming increasingly important. Second, many of these means-tested programs don't give people a hand up, as policy makers profess, but actually have designs that keep people trapped in poverty. Third, social protections for low-income people vary tremendously from state to state, along every conceivable dimension, from the profound (can your baby get health care?) to the trivial (can you get cavities in your molars filled?). It all depends on where you live. Fourth, the many shortcomings of American social policy leave people exposed to tremendous risk. Nowhere else among advanced industrialized democracies can a single accident render you bankrupt, or forever impoverished. Nowhere else can your fate differ so much from one locale to another within the same country. The inadequacies of American social policy set people up for disaster, even those who play by the rules and work hard. Critics allege that social policy is too generous, breeding dependency. In reality, it is often too meager, providing insufficient protections from life's risks. These shortcomings undermine the industriousness and perseverance of citizens like Dave and Marcella. And they cut off opportunities and socioeconomic mobility for both recipients and their children.

1 TRYING TO MAKE IT IN AMERICA

In a beautiful ceremony at the foot of Mount Shasta in Northern California, Dave and Marcella were married in June 2010, just twenty months before the accident. Standing in front of one hundred friends and relatives in our stepmother's backyard, the couple recited vows they had written themselves. Everyone present was thrilled that they had found each other. Dave, a young-at-heart forty-one on their wedding day, had been looking for the right one for a long time. In Marcella, then thirty, he found a smart, beautiful young woman with a keen sense of humor, a demon at games of all types who shared his love of camping and who willingly joined in his avid backpacking and mountain-biking pursuits as well. Both were committed to young people. Marcella had been a counselor for several years at a church camp, and Dave had been taking a couple of unpaid vacation weeks for years to work as a counselor and later codirector of a YMCA summer camp near Mount Lassen. During the wedding reception, over barbecue and a friend's special Wedding Edition home brew, many guests commented on what great parents the couple would make.

Dave and Marcella also had ambitious plans for the future. In particular, they sought a more solid footing in the middle class. Dave very much enjoyed his job, but it didn't offer health insurance or other benefits. The couple planned for Marcella to attend nursing school, capitalizing on the nationwide shortage of nurses and entering one of the few careers promising solid fringe benefits in the economically distressed part of California in which they live. With two incomes, and with the type of employer-provided benefits that signify middle-class financial security, they could pursue a future together—including a family—with confidence.

What Dave and Marcella were keenly aware of—indeed, were arranging their lives around—is that the American welfare state has distinctive tiers, some more attractive, protective, and advantaged than others. Most people most of the time work to make a living, providing themselves and their families with food, housing, clothing, transportation, and other necessities. But life also poses risks to the ability to work: illness, injury, disability, unemployment, and old age. Social insurance programs protect qualifying workers against these risks, providing income and health insurance through workers' compensation, Social Security Disability Insurance, Unemployment Insurance, Social Security retirement benefits, and Medicare. Some workers are additionally protected by the private welfare system of employer-provided benefits, which can include health insurance, short-term disability insurance, paid sick days, retirement savings plans, and so on. But many employers do not offer such benefits. And nonworkers are mostly shut out of both of these systems. When they become sick or disabled or old, they must rely on social assistance programs that generally offer much more meager benefits than either social insurance or the private welfare system. Means-tested social assistance programs are the last resort: people must be poor to qualify for them, and stay poor to continue to receive them.

Dave and Marcella had a plan to move more firmly into the world of social insurance and, better yet, into the privileged world of the private welfare system. Instead, the accident relegated them to the lowest tier of the American welfare state, the social assistance tier, with real questions about whether and how they can escape it. While their story has some especially tragic elements, the financial precariousness and insecurity they endured even before the accident are all too common in the United States.

THE STRUGGLE TO MEET LIFE'S RISKS

I am surrounded by a lot of impressive people at MIT, where I teach, but my brother Dave is one of the smartest people I know. He is a mechanical genius who can make or fix just about anything. He also knows his way around computers, having programmed a number of automated systems at work and created a competitor timing system for the mountain-bike racing circuit in Northern California and beyond. Dave never got a college degree, but he's been able to support himself in a series of steady, if modestly paying jobs. For many years, he's been the manager of a metal fabrication business that engineers and builds parts for houseboats and airplanes.

The company has always been small, and the number of employees has waxed and waned with the state of the economy and the demand for its products. Dave managed to survive the periodic layoffs the company suffered, largely because he could do it all—from front-office payroll, scheduling, and invoicing (he wrote computer programs to automate all these tasks), to bidding, designing, and drafting, to laser cutting and welding on the shop floor. His salary of $39,000 wasn't bad for a single person—just under the US median personal income.[1]

The job came with some considerable perks. Using the laser cutter at work, Dave made a spectacular stainless steel cupcake stand for the wedding, copied from a magazine photograph Marcella had found. But the job didn't come with fringe benefits. No retirement plan, no paid vacation—and no health insurance. Moreover, stretching that income across two, and soon to be three, people would be tight. Dave's salary was well below the US median *household* income of $50,054, coming to only about twice the 2012 federal poverty level for a family of three.[2] It was also below the annual income needed to provide a "secure yet modest living standard" in the Redding, California, area where the couple lives: $60,482 for a family of three, according to the Economic Policy Institute's Family Budget Calculator.[3]

Finding a better-paying job with benefits isn't so easy in Dave and Marcella's geographic area. Shasta County's unemployment rate in 2012 was 14.5 percent—4 points above the California rate, and more than 6 points above the national rate.[4] Jobs with good benefits are rarer still. Just over half of Americans—55 percent—get their health insurance through their employer, while 30 percent are covered by a public program such as Medicare or Medicaid; 16 percent are uninsured. In Shasta County, only 46 percent of its residents have employer-provided health insurance, while 35 percent are covered by a public program.[5] The poverty rate is also high: nearly 18 percent for the county in 2010, compared with 15.8 percent for California and 15.3 percent nationwide.[6]

Despite these odds, Dave and Marcella had mapped a strategy for improving their lot in life: Marcella would get a nursing degree. As one of the few growing careers in their area, just as it is nationwide, nursing promised both a second salary that would place them much more firmly in the middle class and a set of employee benefits that included health insurance, which was the most desirable in their eyes. Marcella already had an undergraduate degree in political science, since she had planned on law school. With her change in career direction, she took her nursing prerequisites at the local community college in preparation for applying to the nursing program there when she finished. Attending part-time, Marcella completed the prereqs in two years. She did so with her characteristic dedication and intelligence, acing every class—even the notoriously difficult anatomy course, which tripped up many other students.

However, there was a hitch in the couple's plans: despite a looming shortage of nurses in the United States—the Bureau of Labor Statistics projects that nursing will be the top occupation for job growth through 2020[7]—there have been far too few slots in nursing programs to meet the demand. Over 75,000 qualified applicants were turned away from nursing programs in 2011 because of budget constraints and shortages of faculty, classroom space, and clinical sites.[8] The local situation paralleled the national one: the community college's nursing program had a two-and-a-half-year waiting list, which an applicant could join only after completing the prereqs. Already over thirty years old and eager to start her new career, Marcella didn't want to wait that long.

She looked to the next alternative, enrolling in the nursing program at California State University, Chico. It would provide a bachelor of science degree in nursing, superior to the associate's degree from the community college. There were downsides to going to Chico, though. The program would cost far more than the community college's, so Marcella would have to take out loans on top of the ones she already had from her first bachelor's degree. On class days, her commute would be a 140-mile round-trip. However, for the promise the degree held, she was willing to make these sacrifices.

But there was yet another hitch. Because of the fiscal crisis in California and the ensuing budget cuts to the state university system, that system imposed a rule to reduce demand: no one who had a BA in another subject would be admitted to its undergraduate programs.

Marcella found the situation deeply disappointing, not to mention nonsensical. Despite a nationwide shortage of nurses, a dedicated young person was being barred from one program and forced to endure a long wait to enter another. In the meantime, Marcella studied to become a phlebotomist; at least that was one way she could start her health care career. Then, just as she was searching for phlebotomy positions, the state university system deemed nursing an impacted field and thus reversed its policy: it lifted the moratorium on admitting those with college degrees. With her outstanding academic record, Marcella was admitted to the nursing program at the Chico campus.

While all this was going on, she searched for health insurance for herself, Dave, and the family they wanted to start soon. Before going back to school, Marcella had health coverage through her job at a bank. Now she and Dave had to shop around in the individual health insurance market. The options weren't great. Marcella received quotes of $1,200 per month—more than the couple's mortgage, more than they could afford—and many of those plans didn't include maternity coverage.[9] Then the search became pressing: when Chico lifted the nursing program moratorium, Marcella needed insurance in order to enroll. The university offered a student health insurance plan, but coverage was limited and the plan required high coinsurance—the patient had to pay 20 percent of all medical bills, and 50 percent for medical care received outside the designated provider network. And then the search grew more pressing still: Marcella became pregnant, a little earlier than planned.

Fortunately, Marcella heard about Access for Infants and Mothers, an insurance program offered by the State of California. AIM provides coverage for middle-income pregnant women who have no health insurance from another source such as an employer, but whose income is too high to qualify for Medicaid/Medi-Cal. In California, Medi-Cal covers the health expenses of pregnant women up to 200 percent of the federal poverty level; those between 200 and 300 percent can qualify for AIM. The cost of the program is 1.5 percent of adjusted annual household income (an affordable total of $585 for Dave and Marcella).

State funding limits AIM enrollment; once the program hits its annual funding cap, even eligible women can't get coverage.[10] Luckily, Marcella was able to enroll, which came as quite a relief. AIM would cover her prenatal visits, delivery, and up to sixty days of postpartum care. Thereafter she would enroll in the Chico State student health plan; she and Dave hoped she'd need only minimal medical care so that the 20 percent coinsurance wouldn't become burdensome. Indeed, before the accident she had already printed out and filled in the application form. The baby would be covered under Healthy Families, California's version of CHIP. Dave and Marcella thought they were prepared. Dave still didn't have coverage, but Marcella and the baby did. The combination of AIM, Healthy Families, and the student plan was serendipitous, and fragmented, but at least it made starting a family possible, despite the couple's lack of access to employer-provided health insurance.[11]

COMMON DIFFICULTIES

Like many Americans, Dave and Marcella didn't live extravagantly. No fancy vacations—mostly camping. No fancy cars—just a 1990 Honda for Marcella and several fixers for Dave, whose hobby was working on old cars. No fancy house—just a twelve-hundred-square-foot ranch style built in 1961; Dave hoped to renovate its original kitchen and bathrooms someday. Things were manageable, but tight.

The couple didn't think of themselves as being in a precarious situation, but their modest wages, limited access to needed education and training programs, and lack of employer-provided benefits and comprehensive health insurance left them vulnerable. And, as with many Americans living with insecurity, a simple misstep, let alone a tragedy, would spell financial disaster.

Low Wages

Part of the insecurity problem in the United States is the prevalence of low-wage work. Officially, one in seven Americans lives in poverty.[12] However, less well known—but perhaps even more consequential—is the fact that the United States also has a large proportion of working poor households. Fully one-third of Americans have "low incomes," meaning incomes below 200 percent of the poverty line; Dave and Marcella are in that group.[13] This working poor population has a difficult time making ends meet. It's also much larger than in other rich nations. Although the per capita gross domestic product (GDP) in the United States is nearly the highest in the world, averaging the economy across all individuals masks the distribution of income, which is highly skewed toward the top end and more skewed than in other advanced economies. A measure that allows for cross-national comparisons—the proportion of full-time workers earning less than 65 percent of the median wage—reveals that one-fourth of Americans earn these low wages, double the proportion in France and Germany and five times the proportion in Sweden and Finland.[14] The United States has a greater percentage of people living in poverty and making low wages than almost all other rich nations.

The situation has worsened. Certainly the Great Recession that began in 2007 took its toll: most of the jobs lost between 2008 and 2010 were middle-wage jobs, while most of the jobs added between 2010 and 2012 were lower-wage jobs.[15] But even before that historic downturn, workers were failing to benefit from increases in economic growth. Worker productivity increased 80 percent between 1973 and 2011, but median hourly compensation grew by only one-eighth that amount in inflation-adjusted terms.[16] Between 2000 and 2011 alone, productivity grew by 23 percent, but workers' wages were flat. Nor have households been spared. With the decline in men's wages that began during the 1970s, women have been flocking to the workplace, shoring up household incomes. But while GDP grew 18 percent from 2000 to 2011, median income for working-age households fell by 12 percent. The reason? Most economic growth during this period accrued not to ordinary workers but to the top 1 percent of earners, who absorbed 65 percent of the nation's income growth between 2002 and 2007.[17] Nor have workers fared well since the Great Recession. In 2012, wages and salaries comprised the smallest share of the GDP since 1929, when such records began, while corporate profits constituted the largest historical share.[18] Lots of Americans like Dave and Marcella work hard but are compensated very modestly. They don't get to share in the economic wealth they helped create.

Unequal Access to Education and Training

One of the best ways for people to increase their income is to get more education or training. Men with bachelor's degrees earn 50 percent more than men with high school degrees.[19] Those with postbaccalaureate degrees earn even more, and the size of this "education wage premium" has increased over time.[20] However, the ability of many Americans, particularly lower-income Americans, to pursue such opportunities has decreased, and the gap in educational attainment across different income groups has grown. In 1970, 40 percent of Americans from families in the top income quartile had a four-year college degree by the age of twenty-four. By 2011, this proportion had grown to 71 percent. In contrast, just 6 percent of those from the bottom income quartile held college degrees in 1970, increasing to only 10 percent by 2011.[21] Sources of federal aid such as Pell Grants have not kept pace with the cost of higher education. As Marcella discovered, budget cuts at many public institutions have put a cap on education and training opportunities—even in areas with looming shortfalls, such as nursing. Government workforce development programs—job training—are scattered across many departments and agencies. The largest program is the Workforce Investment Act under the Labor Department, which spends about $3 billion per year. This may sound like a lot of money, but the Urban Institute estimates that federal funding helps only 5 percent of those who want job training.[22] Private businesses perform far more job training than the government does, but there are worries about underinvestment there as well.

The opportunity gap has widened. Since 1980, the United States has experienced what MIT economist David Autor calls a "polarization" of skills and wages. Employment growth exhibits a U-shaped pattern, with the greatest growth among both high-skill occupations at one end of the spectrum and low-skill service jobs at the other. At the same time, the greatest wage increases have been concentrated at the high end.[23] Unequal access to education and training programs makes it very hard for individuals to upgrade their skills and to enhance their financial prospects. One result is the economic inequality that characterizes contemporary American society.

Lack of Protections from Life's Risks

Beyond low pay is the problem of minimal or nonexistent employer-provided benefits for many members of the American workforce. At one time or another, nearly all workers find themselves in situations where they can't work temporarily or permanently: they are ill, become disabled, lose their job, must care for a child, spouse, or elderly parent, or become too old to work. In many other economically advanced countries, such risks are addressed through public programs: using tax revenues, the government guarantees health insurance to all citizens; family allowances to households with children; paid parental leave for new parents; paid sick leave; paid leave for family caregivers; universal public preschool; retirement pensions; and so on. Such programs take many different forms. Sometimes the government is both the funder and the provider of services; sometimes it pays for the services but contracts with private firms or groups to provide them. No matter the precise arrangement, these public welfare states socialize the costs of life's risks by spreading them across the entire population.

As chapter 3 explores in more depth, the United States has a different approach, a hybrid public-private welfare system. A few risks are socialized through public social welfare programs such as Medicare, which provides health insurance to senior citizens, and Social Security, which provides both retirement pensions to older Americans and disability insurance to qualified workers under the age of sixty-five who can no longer work. However, coverage for many of life's curveballs remains the responsibility of individuals and of families, some of whom are fortunate enough to have employers who provide private benefits that help address these risks. Employers can choose to offer health insurance as well as other benefits such as a traditional pension or 401(k) retirement savings program, paid parental leave, paid sick days, short-term disability payments, maternity leave, paid vacation, and so on. But offering such benefits is completely optional for employers. They aren't required by law to do so.

Lack of Health Insurance

One of the most important benefits is health insurance. The United States is just about the only industrialized country in the world that doesn't guarantee health insurance for its citizens (Belarus and the former Balkan states are the other exceptions). Employer-provided insurance is optional—and expensive for both employer and employee. Nonetheless, it remains the primary source of health coverage: in 2011, about 55 percent of Americans had employer-provided insurance, while 16.5 percent had Medicaid coverage and 15.2 percent were covered by Medicare (people can have more than one type of insurance).[24] A small proportion purchased insurance on the individual market, but such plans are often difficult to obtain and are expensive. Nearly 16 percent lacked health insurance altogether.[25] That's 50 million people, one-sixth of the country's population, the combined populations of these twenty-three states: Oklahoma, Connecticut, Iowa, Mississippi, Arkansas, Kansas, Utah, Nevada, New Mexico, West Virginia, Nebraska, Idaho, Hawaii, Maine, New Hampshire, Rhode Island, Montana, Delaware, South Dakota, Alaska, North Dakota, Vermont, and Wyoming.

Most Americans without health insurance live in households that have at least one worker. And most Americans whose employer offers health insurance enroll in it—84 percent in 2010. But over time, fewer employers have offered health insurance.[26] And the smaller the employer, the less likely it is to do so. In 2011, more than one-third of workers in small firms like Dave's with fewer than ten employees were uninsured, compared with just one in seven workers in large companies of one thousand or more.[27]

Insurance coverage also varies with age, income, and education. Because of Medicare, the uninsurance rate is lowest among the elderly, less than 2 percent in 2011. In contrast, among those aged twenty-six to thirty-four years—Marcella's age group—28 percent lacked insurance in 2011.[28] The uninsurance rate declines with income also. In Dave and Marcella's income group—households with incomes from $25,000 to $50,000—22 percent were uninsured, about 6 points above the overall uninsurance rate, while less than 8 percent of those with incomes over $65,000 were uninsured.[29] Over 80 percent of the college educated were offered employer-based health benefits in 2010, compared with just 64 percent of those with high school educations.[30]

On top of the 50 million uninsured Americans, another 25 million are underinsured, potentially exposed to substantial out-of-pocket costs.[31] Underinsurance can result from hospital-only coverage that leaves individuals liable for any procedure done on an outpatient basis, which nowadays includes the majority of surgeries and chemotherapy. It can also result from insurance plans that cover only a fraction of hospital costs or have no limit on out-of-pocket expenses, which can rack up quickly with a major illness or chronic condition.[32] Partly because of widespread underinsurance, medical debt is an important cause of personal bankruptcy in the United States, even among the insured. Medical costs contribute to bankruptcy both directly, through the uncovered medical bills themselves, and indirectly, through the loss of income from illness. Many of those with insurance at the onset of illness ultimately declare bankruptcy because they lost their coverage due to job problems, leaving them liable for the full cost of their care.[33] Bankruptcies tend to have multiple causes, so it is difficult to measure precisely the effect of medical debt.[34] But we do know that this pattern of events—illness, job loss, insurance loss, bankruptcy—is uniquely American.[35] In virtually all other economically advanced nations, citizens have health insurance regardless of their employment situation.

The Obama administration health reform, the Affordable Care Act, will cut the number of uninsured and underinsured and will reduce some—but not all—disparities in health insurance coverage by age, income, and education, as chapter 6 explains. In other countries, however, these differences in insurance coverage across subgroups do not exist. People have health coverage by virtue of their citizenship.

INSECURITY AS THE NEW NORMAL

Apart from the economic elite, many Americans live precariously. Millions work in jobs with no fringe benefits. The minimum wage is not a living wage in most parts of the country.[36] One in three households lives below 200 percent of the poverty level, itself below the income needed for a "modest living standard" in most parts of the country.[37] Savings are quite modest for many: among households with incomes below $25,000 in 2005, two-thirds had no or only low emergency savings ($500 or less); nearly 40 percent of households between $25,000 and $50,000 in income had virtually no cash savings.[38] Nearly all these trends have worsened: real wages are flat or declining for many; fewer employers offer benefits, including health insurance; education and training access is declining. Financial insecurity is growing.

Consider the situation of middle-income families. Couples have been responding to flat individual earnings by putting second earners into the workforce: three-fourths of mothers with children under the age of eighteen worked outside the home in 2010, while less than half did in 1975.[39] However, two-earner households are in worse shape now than one-earner households were in 1970. Back then, the nonworking spouse was a source of insurance for the family: she (usually she) could enter the paid workforce if the breadwinner lost his job; between her new wages and his unemployment benefits, family income would drop only slightly. But now, with families dependent on two incomes to begin with, and fewer people eligible for Unemployment Insurance (see chapter 3), job loss is a catastrophe. It results in a 29 percent drop in pretax income for the household, and a 77 percent decline in discretionary income (what's left over after the mortgage, child care, health insurance, car expenses, and taxes).[40] Even during "good times," today's families are worse off financially: because the cost of health insurance and the cost of housing in neighborhoods with good schools have risen so much, two-earner households now have less discretionary income than did one-earner households in 1970.[41]

THE UPHILL STRUGGLE

Before the accident, Dave and Marcella had resembled many families in the United States. Like tens of millions of other Americans, Dave worked for an employer that didn't offer health insurance. His full-time wages in manufacturing left his family at just three-fourths of the median household income. Like the vast majority of couples, including those with young children, Dave and Marcella had concluded that both partners would have to work to make ends meet. In their case, Marcella sought one of the few jobs in their area that promised employer-provided benefits: nursing. But despite strong occupational demand, like many others she faced hurdle after hurdle in pursuit of that dream.

Dave and Marcella didn't have it easy, but they did have a plan. And they had the advantages of youth, energy, and a strong commitment to each other. They would forge a new, more secure life for themselves and for their new baby, even if it meant short-term sacrifice.

Then disaster struck, and our family learned how truly difficult it is to make it in America.

DOWN
THE RABBIT
HOLE

After the accident, Marcella was airlifted to the main regional hospital, Mercy Medical Center in Redding. Our family knows Mercy well: Dave's and my late father had delivered thousands of babies there as an ob-gyn; he also served two terms as the chief of medical staff and later was chief medical officer and regional vice president.

In the days immediately after the accident, Dave lived at the hospital, sleeping in Marcella's room in the intensive care unit on one of those torturous chair-bed combos usually reserved for expectant fathers in labor-and-delivery rooms. He went upstairs to the neonatal intensive care unit to see the baby when he could. Logan was doing great, gaining weight, looking cool in the sunglasses he wore when getting ultraviolet light treatments for his jaundice. In contrast, Marcella suffered a series of scary setbacks. The reality of her long, long road ahead sunk in. Dave was doing remarkably well, though, considering that all their plans lay in shambles, and that rather than juggling a newborn, a job, and a wife in school, he was contemplating a future in which he must somehow make a living while caring for an infant and a permanently disabled spouse. I plied him with coffee, and we had long talks in the hospital cafeteria, where doctors and nurses who had known Dad came over to offer their support.

WE LEARN HOW MEDI-CAL REALLY WORKS

Dave mentioned the things he'd been hearing in the days since the accident—that Marcella's health care would be covered by Medi-Cal but also, "You'll have to get rid of everything," "You'll have to declare bankruptcy," and, more helpfully, "Go talk to Brian—he's the Medi-Cal guru." Brian (not his real name) is the medical center's social worker who handles the Medi-Cal cases. He met us to begin to explain how the program works.

From my social policy work, I knew that Medi-Cal is California's version of Medicaid, the public health insurance program for the poor. Medicaid was enacted in 1965, part of the same legislation that created Medicare, the public health insurance program for older Americans. Medicare is a federal program, which means that eligibility and benefit levels are the same nationwide. In contrast, Medicaid is run jointly by the federal government and the states. The federal government pays part of the cost of Medicaid and requires that every state cover several "mandatory populations," such as poor children and pregnant women and most disabled and elderly people eligible for Supplemental Security Income, the federal cash assistance program for the poor disabled, blind, or aged.[1]

Brian, patient and soft-spoken, began to explain what would happen with Marcella's hospital bills. The Access for Infants and Mothers program in which she had enrolled for her pregnancy would pay some of the bills for the first sixty days postpartum. Medi-Cal would pay the others, and then would be Marcella's sole insurance after the AIM coverage ran out.[2]

Brian continued: Marcella qualified for Medi-Cal because she is disabled, but because Medi-Cal is for poor people, Dave and Marcella have to be poor to receive it—they have to "meet" the program's "income test." Counterintuitively, meeting the income test doesn't mean having enough income (as in doing well on a test), but rather having low-enough income. The income test is actually an income limit.

Moreover, because Dave is employed, he and Marcella would be in a particular version of the program called "Share of Cost" Medi-Cal. It works this way: as a family of three with one disabled member, they are allowed to keep $2,100 of Dave's $3,250 monthly earnings to live on. The rest of Dave's earnings, $1,150, would go to Medi-Cal as the family's share of cost. That is, any month in which Marcella incurred medical expenses, she and Dave must pay the first $1,150. To our surprise, if Dave earned more money, the extra amount would also go to Medi-Cal: the cost sharing is a 100 percent tax on Dave's earnings. I figured out later that the $2,100 my brother and sister-in-law are to live on puts them at 133 percent of the federal poverty level for a family of three. Essentially, the way they meet the income test is for Medi-Cal to skim off Dave's income until they are in fact poor. Brian noted that they are "lucky" that they are allowed to retain that much income; if Marcella weren't disabled, the amount they'd be allowed to retain would be even lower than $2,100. And this is how things will be indefinitely. In order to get poor people's health insurance, Dave and Marcella must stay poor, forever.

Stunned, Dave and I listened in silence. How are they going to raise a child at the poverty level?

I tried to think what I could do. "In a couple of years, as the baby's aunt, can I pay for preschool?"

"If it were considered a loan, yes. But if you simply pay for his preschool, it counts as income for Dave and Marcella, so no, you can't do that." Brian paused as that sank in. "Of course, if you happen to show up at their house with a carful of groceries, no one will know."[3]

Later, Dave and I stood in the hallway outside the ICU. I pulled out a notebook, and we started listing his and Marcella's monthly expenses. Mortgage and property taxes: $1,000. Utilities: $200. Phones and Internet: $180. Homeowners, auto, and life insurance: $225. Gas: $200. Logan's Healthy Families insurance premium: $45. We quickly approached $2,100, but hadn't yet included clothing, or toiletries, or Marcella's college loans. Or payments on the wheelchair van they will need. Or food.

With this information in hand, when Dave returned to work a few months after the accident, he pared his hours down to meet the $2,100 level: why work more when it would all go to Medi-Cal? He and Marcella struggled to make ends meet on that near-poverty income. And then much later, at the time I was writing this book, we discovered that he probably didn't need to reduce his pay; he and Marcella were probably not subject to a Share of Cost requirement even at Dave's pre-accident income, a revelation to which I will return. But we didn't know that for two years. And the income limits are only part of the difficulty of living under Medi-Cal. We next learned about Medi-Cal's other strictures, limits that do apply to Dave and Marcella, and that are even more Draconian.

Back in Brian's office, we heard that Dave and Marcella must also meet Medi-Cal's asset test. As with the income test, passing the test doesn't mean doing well or reaching a certain high level: the asset "test" is an asset limit. Their house and one vehicle are exempt. Beyond those two items, they can possess only $3,150 in assets, total. They have to liquidate everything else[4] and must put the resulting cash only into the house and the one vehicle. They can't use the money to pay household bills, credit card bills, or Marcella's student loans. They will have to save every receipt to prove how the money was spent.

The asset test requires them to cash in the small 401(k) account Marcella had started when she worked at the bank (and, adding insult to injury, pay the early withdrawal penalty). They have to spend down their bank account. Even Dave's hobby runs afoul of the asset test: he must sell the old cars he was working on.

I sat there wondering how they were going to fashion a life for themselves on $3,150 in assets. These social policies for the poor are no hand up, as many politicians would have us believe. Marcella and Dave aren't allowed to save for retirement (retirement plans aren't exempt from the asset test in California as they are in some states). They can't establish an emergency fund in case the water heater breaks or they need a new roof. They can't save for Logan's college education with a tax-free 529 plan—California is one of twenty-four states that haven't exempted such plans from their Medicaid asset tests—although two other, less attractive college savings vehicles are still available to them.[5]

In sum, they are barred from doing many of the things middle-class families are constantly advised to do: Save for retirement. Save for emergencies. Take advantage of tax-free college savings plans. Just $3,150 in total assets—that's it.

Brian added, "You're lucky—without the baby, the asset limit would be $3,000."

Later, I found out that the asset limit was last changed in 1989.

Brian saw the look on our faces. "Medi-Cal is a poor person's program," he said with a shrug. "And it's not really even insurance—it's a loan." Thus, any inheritances Dave and Marcella might receive will go to Medi-Cal. Any Medi-Cal services that Marcella uses after the age of fifty-five will be added to a tab that she will rack up over the rest of her life; when she and my brother die, the state will make a claim on their estate for reimbursement, as Logan will no longer be a minor at that point.[6] He will inherit nothing.

My brother and I said nothing as we walked out of Brian's office and headed back upstairs to the ICU. Each of us was processing the awful news: Dave and Marcella faced a lifetime of financial insecurity to get the medical care she needs.

MEDI-CAL'S LIMITS

We got our first taste of Medi-Cal's limits as an insurance program when Marcella's condition was stable enough for her to be transferred from the ICU to a rehabilitation hospital. As poor people's insurance, Medicaid is a poor payer. Its reimbursements to physicians and hospitals are generally lower than those under Medicare or private insurance. As a result, many health care providers are reluctant to accept Medicaid patients.[7] Moreover, among state Medicaid programs, Medi-Cal is a particularly low payer.[8] This became a problem for Marcella as the day approached for her release from the acute care hospital to a rehabilitative setting. The closest facility that specialized in spinal cord injuries was in the Bay Area, a four-hour drive away. Although the prospect of being so far from home was daunting, more problematic was the facility's hesitancy to admit Marcella. It wants to make sure that each new patient is willing to work hard and will be worthy of one of the limited rehab slots. A nurse drove up to Redding to evaluate Marcella, and saw that she's a determined young woman—definitely a good candidate for the facility's services. But it also wanted to make sure she was completely stabilized and strong enough to breathe on her own before starting the demanding rehab regimen. We got the impression that Medi-Cal would pay for only one month of rehab, so Marcella had to be completely ready when the time came.

In the meantime, Logan was released from the neonatal intensive care unit after two weeks. Although born several weeks premature, he was unharmed by the accident ("I was his human airbag," Marcella says). At this point he just needed to keep growing and gaining weight, which he could safely do outside the hospital. Dave's and my mother came out from Minnesota, where she had retired a few years prior, to care for Logan. While Marcella remained in the ICU for several more weeks, Mom and Logan stayed in a spare bedroom at the home of one of Marcella's brothers.

Now out of the hospital, however, Logan needed a physician. Several members of Marcella's family had long seen Dr. S, a charismatic and well-liked general practitioner in town. Marcella had known him since she was ten years old, and hoped he would be Logan's physician as well. But Dr. S doesn't accept Healthy Families, because it's a low payer.[9] The ICU nurses gave Marcella the names of several good pediatricians at the local county clinic, the public facility that takes Healthy Families and Medi-Cal. But Marcella was intent on having Dr. S, who, given the circumstances, relented. He promised to see Logan for his well-baby visits, waiving his personal fee, although Dave and Marcella still had to pay the office portion of the charge out of pocket. For any other services or procedures, such as vaccines, they would have to go to the county clinic.

Except that's not so easy either. Because Logan was born prematurely, he was susceptible to respiratory syncytial virus and was supposed to get a monthly injection of RSV antibodies until winter was over. He got his first one in the hospital, but needed one more after he was discharged. Dr. S's office wouldn't give the injection, but said that County would. Dave bundled Logan off to the county clinic, only to find that it didn't have the vaccine. Dave was told to get it from the pharmacist, and then the clinic would give the injection. But Dave didn't have Logan's Healthy Family card yet, and the pharmacist wouldn't sell him the vaccine for cash, saying that he had to have insurance to get the vaccine; otherwise it constitutes fraud. Dave found that puzzling, but moot: the shot cost $800, which Dave wasn't about to pay. The pharmacy was eventually able to get approval for the vaccine from Medi-Cal, and ended up giving Logan the shot in its own flu clinic. So the baby did get his shot, but not before a delay and a confusing runaround—certainly not the last one the family would encounter.

REHAB

Marcella dreaded the four-hour drive to the rehab hospital in the Bay Area. Her neck wasn't completely healed where doctors had surgically stabilized it after the accident. The prospect of traveling on a freeway again terrified her. Then, in an act of kindness, Mercy Medical Center donated an air ambulance ride, so she flew to the Bay Area instead.

Marcella stayed in the rehab hospital for three months. It took longer to stabilize her breathing than anticipated—she also wasn't able to speak for a while due to injured vocal cords, and spent the first two months in the spinal cord ICU—but eventually she attended daily physical therapy sessions and met with a phalanx of social workers and therapists. Mom, Marcella's mother, and Logan moved into a small apartment adjacent to the hospital that family members rent for a nominal fee. Dave again slept in Marcella's hospital room. He and other family members who could travel down to the Bay Area learned how to perform her daily care. Dave quickly became a great favorite of the hospital staff, not only for his quick learning and witticisms but also for his formidable mechanical skills. He rigged up a Camelbak water reservoir with a special wire to bring the drinking tube close to Marcella's mouth. That way, she could easily sip and stay hydrated, a necessity for quadriplegics. He noticed a machine in her room that often made a hissing noise. "It always does that. It's incredibly annoying, but we learn to ignore it," a nurse told him. He repurposed a coupling and a short tube from the respiratory department that solved the problem. In days, all the patients in the unit had them. No more hissing. The nurses loved him for that.

RETURNING HOME

After three months in the rehab facility, Dave and Marcella returned to Redding. Medi-Cal's limitations once again became apparent. They left the hospital with a bag of prescriptions, but discovered that Medi-Cal will pay for only six prescriptions per month. They have to pay for the others out of pocket. One of the uncovered drugs prevents the accumulation of calcium in Marcella's joints (when a bone breaks, as several of Marcella's had during the accident, the body produces extra calcium to heal the fracture, and any excess gets reabsorbed; however, if the person is paralyzed and can't move, the excess calcium tends to deposit in joints). She had started this drug's course in the hospital but couldn't afford the rest, so she did without it upon release, hoping for no negative effect. Later on, she staggered her medications to stay under the monthly limit, but continued to pay out of pocket for a blood-pressure-stabilizing medicine—the drug in the class that Medi-Cal would cover leaches potassium from the body, which is bad for the heart.

Back in Redding, Dave, Mom, and Logan moved into our step-mom's house, and Marcella lived with her parents as she and Dave waited for a friend-and-family-initiated remodeling of their house to be completed. They adjusted to life outside the cocoon of twenty-four-hour medical care. Beyond the immediate daily struggles to perform Marcella's care and keep the baby occupied were the new realities of life. How would Marcella get the equipment and the personal care services she needed? How would they manage life's surprises with virtually no savings? The complexity of the system they must navigate from now on is almost unbelievable. Back at Mercy, I had drawn up a list of all the programs we had to keep tabs on, and Dave and I had gone to an office supply store to get him a portable file box. He needed to get Logan's Healthy Families application going. He had to tell AIM when the baby was born so it could begin to count the sixty days of postpartum care it would cover. He needed to file for Unemployment Insurance or California paid family leave for the period he would be out of work. In the early days, we had so many questions about Marcella's eligibility for various programs. Medicare? No. Medi-Cal? Yes. SSDI? No. SSI? Yes. IHSS—what's that? I thought Dave's head would explode. It was impossible for any single person, even nondisabled, to navigate the entire, immensely complicated system alone. Marcella's sister and sister-in-law divvied up the programs, got permission to act as her proxy, and began figuring everything out.

American public social programs run on two tracks: social insurance for workers and social assistance for the poor. It turns out that Marcella isn't eligible for the programs of the "upper" social insurance track. She hadn't worked enough quarters before going back to school to be an insured worker. She hadn't paid into Social Security long enough to be eligible for Social Security Disability Insurance, the monthly cash benefit for the permanently disabled. Nor had she paid into Medicare long enough to be eligible for that form of public health insurance (after a two-year waiting period, SSDI recipients can go on Medicare). As a nonworker, she is eligible only for the means-tested programs—Medicaid/Medi-Cal for health insurance and SSI for cash assistance.

I was devastated when I first realized Marcella was outside the social insurance track. SSDI benefits are typically larger than SSI benefits. Medicare is more widely accepted by physicians and hospitals than Medicaid. I thought her ineligibility was a disaster. And it is: Dave and Marcella will have to stay on the social assistance track forever for her to get health insurance. But as it turns out, even if she had another source of health insurance, the social assistance track is inevitable for her: there's no other source for the lifelong services the disabled need, especially for personal care assistants. Medicare doesn't cover long-term care. Private health insurance doesn't cover it. There is a tiny market of private long-term care insurance, but as chapter 3 explains, it's a highly flawed insurance product, almost no one Marcella's age has it, and it won't cover a lifetime of need. Thus, well beyond Marcella's health insurance needs are her long-term personal assistance needs. For those, Medicaid is essentially the only alternative. And so, the poverty track it is.

In-Home Support Services (IHSS) is the California program that pays for personal care assistance for Medi-Cal recipients, allowing the disabled, the aged, and the blind who would otherwise go into a nursing home to remain in their own homes (note that *long-term care* [LTC] is an older but still common term connoting more medicalized care, often used with regard to the elderly, while the newer *long-term services and supports* [LTSS] is preferred by the disability community, indicating the supports that allow the disabled to live independently at home).[10] Beginning in the 1990s, many states secured waivers from Medicaid regulations so that they were permitted to use Medicaid money not just for institutional care but also for care provided in the home, such as IHSS.[11] Although funded by federal, state, and county money, the IHSS program is run by the county, which sent a social worker to evaluate Marcella's needs.

IHSS services can include personal care (such as bowel and bladder care, bathing, grooming, and paramedical services) as well as household tasks (housecleaning, meal preparation, laundry, grocery shopping) and accompaniment to medical appointments.[12] Because of the extent of her paralysis, Marcella qualified for the maximum number of care hours. She also received some additional hours from another program called In Home Operations, for a total of thirteen per day. Home care workers' wages are set by the county; Shasta County IHSS care workers earned $9.30 per hour in 2012[13] (a wage rate that ironically leaves a full-time care worker him- or herself below the poverty line for a family of three). Alternatively, if Marcella's family members take on the care, they too can be paid, as is the case in a number of states. They would have to fill out time cards, which Marcella would need to approve and then submit to the county. However, even though Marcella receives the maximum number of hours of care, Dave must still handle all her care at night when they are together, and wakes every five hours to do so. I worry that he'll never get a full night's sleep again.

Beyond personal care attendants, a disabled person like Marcella

needs medical equipment such as a wheelchair, incontinence supplies, and assistive technologies, not to mention an accessible place
to live and a wheelchair van for transportation. Public assistance for
these needs is extremely spotty. Medicaid will pay for incontinence
supplies, although fewer than Marcella actually needs; every month
she has to apply and get approval for thirty additional catheters.
Medicaid will pay for a wheelchair, although not necessarily an adequate one. The rehab facility social worker doubted Medi-Cal would
pay for a fully reclining wheelchair, and ordered a partial-tilt one instead. Now when Marcella has to be catheterized every five hours, she
has to stop what's she's doing and go home to a bed where she can
lie flat. Later, her rehab physician in Redding wrote her caseworker,
saying that Marcella needs a reclining wheelchair. After six months,
no response.

In contrast, Medicare will fund only some of these items, and then
only with the patient paying 20 percent coinsurance. Such coinsurance can be substantial—electric wheelchairs for quadriplegics can
run $10,000 to $30,000 or more, the special cushions and chair backs
hundreds or thousands of dollars additional.

Quite often, people can't procure needed equipment through the
public health insurance programs, but rather rely on a patchwork of
advocacy and charitable organizations that are trying to fill the gaps.
Prominent among these are Centers for Independent Living, nonprofit organizations run by and for people with disabilities.[14] CILs are
nonresidential facilities that assist the disabled with daily living issues. They provide housing information, peer counseling, personal
assistant services, independent living skills training, legal aid, assistive technology services, employment readiness training, benefits
counseling, and referrals.[15] The staff of the Independent Living Services of Northern California (the Redding/Chico CIL), which recycles
and redistributes assistive technologies, were wonderfully helpful.
They contacted us shortly after the accident, and offered their "library" of beds, lifts, and other equipment.

Accessible housing and transportation is another matter altogether. Some states allow Medicaid dollars to pay for items such as

grab bars, wheelchair ramps, and bath seats.[16] But those are small potatoes. There's essentially no help in the United States for purchasing the big-ticket item: accessibility renovations to the home, which can cost tens of thousands of dollars. Disability activist Michael Ogg, whose story is in chapter 3, spent $150,000 making his home accessible, entirely out of his own pocket. Nor is there any help at all to get a wheelchair van. Dave and I looked online: a used one costs $25,000.

Dave and Marcella don't have that kind of money, but their community has been extraordinarily generous. Fortunately, the home Dave bought years ago is one story and just two steps above street level, but it had small rooms, narrow hallways, and tight corners. An architect from a nearby community who had experienced temporary paralysis volunteered his expertise in creating a new floor plan with a more open design. The weekend after the accident, when Marcella's baby shower was to have had been held, friends and relatives were packing all the couple's belongings and moving them to the storage facility run by Marcella's oldest brother. The crew of family and friends gutted the house and began the renovation. A local construction company offered to coordinate the subcontracting, and some materials were donated. Local vendors offered many other items at cost. All over town, people held fund-raisers for Dave and Marcella. Marcella's brothers set up an account at a local bank and an online fund-raising campaign—but in *their* names, so that the collected funds wouldn't interfere with Marcella's eligibility for Medi-Cal and the other public programs (all the money went to the house anyway). Dave and Marcella bought a wheelchair van, but with their limited resources they ended up financing it, and the monthly payments continue to threaten their budget. But at least they could see their new lives taking shape.

The outpouring of support from the local community has been astounding. But the feeling of being hunted has been too. Just one example: A local café fell behind on its taxes. Rather than see it close down, loyal patrons held a fund-raiser, which happened to take place shortly after Marcella's accident. The café owner told the local newspaper she would give Marcella any extra funds raised.

This was a lovely, humane gesture. Only problem is, the social worker reads the paper too. After the fund-raiser, she called up: *Where's the money?* A lump sum could violate Dave and Marcella's asset test. I think: It's all going toward the house! If we had to pay a contractor to do the renovation, it would cost $150,000. You should be happy we're doing it on a shoestring. *That's* where the money is going.[17]

At any rate, Dave and Marcella began to figure out how all the other pieces of their lives were going to work. Marcella couldn't breast-feed Logan because of her medications, a huge disappointment to her. She and the baby did qualify for Women, Infants and Children, the supplemental nutritional program for lower-income pregnant and breast-feeding women, infants, and children under the age of five. WIC supplies infant formula, but only one type, which made Logan throw up. Our stepmom got him the Costco brand, which went down better. I wondered what people who don't have middle-class relatives do in a situation like this.

Dave needed to figure out a way to get to his job. The wheelchair van is his and Marcella's exempt vehicle; any other vehicle counts against their Medicaid asset limit. Among the old cars Dave was working on, he decided to keep a 1968 Datsun pickup, because its value is just a few hundred dollars. It's forty-five years old and weighs 2,200 pounds, less than a Miata sports car. It has no modern safety features. So the only able-bodied adult in the household will have to drive an unsafe car to work. And he can't transport Logan in it because it has no backseat.

Then there was the child care conundrum. Mom had come from Minnesota to care for Logan. But she couldn't stay forever—who would care for him after she left? And with what funds? I dreaded the day Mom would need to go home.

Finally, I worried about Dave. He had so much on his plate. I hoped the stress wasn't sending his blood pressure up. He spent all his time in hospitals, surrounded by medical personnel, tending to everyone else—I wished *he* would see a doctor.

MYSTERY HOUSE

And then we found out that one crucial piece of information we had learned about Medi-Cal was wrong. In January 2014, nearly two years after the accident, I was fact-checking this book. I got access to state-level Medi-Cal officials, who pulled up Marcella's records and told me that she wasn't enrolled in Share of Cost Medi-Cal. She was in SSI-linked Medi-Cal. So her health insurance is free. She has no Share of Cost requirement.

No caseworker had ever mentioned this crucial fact. Who knows when we would have stumbled upon it had I not written this book. But then the key question became: If Dave returned to his pre-accident income of $3,250 per month, would Marcella still be eligible for free Medi-Cal? Or would they be subject to Share of Cost and back in the same boat? Medi-Cal officials wouldn't tell me, and referred me to the calculators on the World Institute on Disability website.[18]

From what I could discern, at Dave's pre-accident income Marcella's SSI would decrease and even disappear, but she'd still be eligible for free Medi-Cal under a different program, Aged and Disabled Federal Poverty Level Medi-Cal. However, if Dave's income increased much above that level, Marcella would get kicked into a third program, Aged, Blind, Disabled Medically Needy Medi-Cal, which *does* have a Share of Cost, which would likely drive their net income right back down again.[19]

It appears, then, that Dave and Marcella didn't have to trim their income down to the 133 percent of poverty level we'd thought, but they can't go much above 200 percent without triggering Share of Cost Medi-Cal—still below what's needed for a modest living standard budget. I can't be completely sure of this, but it also seems that they had lived for two years on a lower income than necessary. Could we approach Marcella's caseworker to run the what-if scenarios and see how much income Dave could earn without threatening her eligibility? No, state officials told me: county caseworkers are incredibly busy, particularly with Medi-Cal expansion under the Affordable Care

Act. This would be a low-priority request. Just look at the calculators and figure it out, they advised.

But I can't—not with any certainty, to my enormous frustration. So much for helping my brother and sister-in-law navigate the system. Medi-Cal is a collection of over one hundred programs, each with its own income methodology and rules. A person familiar with Medi-Cal likened the program to the Winchester Mystery House, the San Jose mansion constructed continually over four decades by the odd widow of the Winchester rifle fortune: there is no master plan. "All the 'rooms' added on over the years makes it very difficult to see which rules apply to which groups and to follow them all the way through," this observer told me. And even if Dave and Marcella could retain a bit more income to live on, they are still subject to the asset limit and all of Medi-Cal's other strictures. They are still trapped in an eccentric's mansion, where the stairways lead to ceilings and the doors open onto walls.

THE ROTTEN CORE

Without Medi-Cal, Dave and Marcella would be liable for enormous medical bills. Even if they'd had private health insurance in this pre–Affordable Care Act world, they probably would have exceeded the annual cap and perhaps even the lifetime cap (a limit on the amount an insurer will pay out) before her ICU and rehabilitation hospital stays were over. I never did find out the total bill, but when we talked to Brian the social worker about a week after the accident, his computer screen showed the ticker for Marcella's and Logan's ICU stays up to that point: $474,000 for Marcella, $111,000 for Logan. The baby spent another week in the NICU, while Marcella was in the Mercy ICU for three more weeks, followed by the three-month rehabilitation hospital stay. With private insurance, even if they didn't hit annual or lifetime caps, Marcella and Dave may well have had a 20 percent co-insurance requirement, which would have totaled hundreds of thousands of dollars. Either way, they would have had to have declared bankruptcy.

At its center, American social policy has a rotten core: incomplete protections from life's risks. For Dave and Marcella, private insurance would have meant bankruptcy (while the ACA removes annual and lifetime caps, large out-of-pocket expenses remain a possibility). Medi-Cal means dire financial straits for the rest of their lives. It's instructive to read through the heartbreaking stories on other people's online medical fund-raising pages—so many face similar horrible situations, including many who thought they had good health insurance until a catastrophic accident or expensive medical condition proved otherwise. And for those readers who think Dave and Marcella are irresponsible loafers who are soaking the public (after I wrote about their situation in the *New York Times*, I received several such e-mails), consider the issue of long-term care.[20] Almost no one has private coverage for that. Certainly not at the age of thirty-two, and not for decades' worth of care. When disaster strikes, the holes in the American system of social protections become woefully apparent.

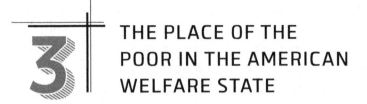

THE PLACE OF THE POOR IN THE AMERICAN WELFARE STATE

Here's a puzzle: Dave and I grew up in the same upper-middle-class family. Our dad was a prominent doctor in town. Indeed, his name is etched in the glass on one of the ICU rooms at Mercy Medical Center, where Marcella had stayed after the accident. And yet when Dave's wife and baby needed treatment in our dad's hospital, they couldn't get it without resorting to a means-tested program. Dave had to shed his assets to secure their care, and will now live in a state of financial vulnerability and anxiety for the rest of his life. How does the American welfare state allow this to happen?

Dave and Marcella's situation illustrates the tremendous separation between the distinct layers of American social policy. The poor make do with the lowest level, the social assistance tier of means-tested programs, where Dave and Marcella now find themselves because of the accident. In this tier, benefits tend to be low, and many have deteriorated over time. Recipients have to fight to establish eligibility and to get what they need. They can't accept assistance from family members without violating eligibility criteria. And they must remain poor to remain in the programs.

As a worker, Dave (but not Marcella) qualifies for the next tier up, the social insurance programs such as Social Security and Medicare. Benefits are higher in this tier and, particularly for Social Security, are designed to keep up with inflation. They aren't means-tested, so beneficiaries in this tier can supplement the public benefit with private insurance and personal savings, and they can accept help from family members without penalty. And, especially for Social Security and Medicare, benefits are not stigmatized; indeed, the system is set up to get recipients the maximum benefits for which they qualify.

I am luckier still, for I benefit not only from the social insurance programs for jobholders like Dave but also from the highest tier of the American welfare state, the private welfare system of employer-provided benefits. These can include a variety of protections such as health insurance and retirement pensions. However, whether an employer offers them is their choice. That mine does and Dave's doesn't means that we enjoy very different levels of financial security—and had done so even before the accident. That's because the private welfare system isn't available to all—employer-provided benefits are more common in higher-level, higher-paid jobs. And while we call this system private, it has a big public component: it's heavily subsidized by the tax break system.

All modern industrialized democracies have a *welfare state*, a "collection of programs designed to assure economic security to all citizens by guaranteeing the fundamental necessities of life: food, shelter, medical care, protection in childhood, support in old age."[1] What sets the United States apart is that few of these protections are actually provided to *all* citizens. Which protections we enjoy depends on whether we work, and for whom. Many Americans must do without vital aspects of security like health insurance, or in desperation must enter the means-tested tier when there are no alternatives.

Indeed, readers may think Marcella and Dave's descent from the middle class to Medi-Cal is a rare misfortune, but that's not the case. This chapter shows that a majority of Americans will use a means-tested social program at some point during their working years, due to low and volatile incomes and a lack of employer-provided benefits. It also shows how differently people fare in the various tiers of the American welfare state. What happens when you're a worker whose employer doesn't offer benefits? What happens when you aren't a jobholder at all? Mostly, the poor get the short end of the stick, even those who are employed.

THE SURPRISINGLY WIDESPREAD USE
OF MEANS-TESTED PROGRAMS

Most Americans work hard. Few would view themselves as prospective recipients of social assistance programs. After all, aren't most people in means-tested programs the chronically poor? And aren't stories such as Marcella and Dave's sad but rare?

In truth, most people will encounter these programs at some point in their lives. Between the ages of twenty-five and sixty-five, two-thirds of Americans will live in a household that receives food stamps, Medicaid, Supplemental Security Income (SSI), or Temporary Assistance for Needy Families (TANF) or other cash welfare.[2] In 2012, one in seven Americans received food stamps, including one in four children. Medicaid funds 40 percent of all births in the United States.[3] Social assistance programs aren't marginal—they're mainstream.

Indeed, one day I remarked to my husband that we had received a means-tested program. "We did? When was that?" I reminded him that when we were expecting our first child, we needed to move because our landlords, who lived upstairs, prohibited children (in Massachusetts, landlords in owner-occupied two- or three-family houses can bar pretty much anyone they want). The problem was finding a de-leaded apartment. The housing stock in the Boston area is old, with a lot of lead paint that children can accidentally ingest when fine particles float to the floor with the opening and closing of windows and doors. Under Massachusetts law, landlords are liable for lead poisoning claims, so many won't rent to families unless they have de-leaded units, which are few and expensive. Fortunately for us, the City of Cambridge had sponsored a de-leading program, installing new windows and doors for landlords who were then required to rent to young families. We located such an apartment, and because I was in grad school and my husband was a lecturer in the arts, we fell under the income guideline: it was a means-tested program.

Political rhetoric encourages us to think of "welfare versus work," but in reality the two often coincide. Recall that one-third of American households have incomes below 200 percent of the federal poverty level. Many of these folks qualify for means-tested programs. I know a couple, a small-town schoolteacher and a part-time public health nurse, who were nonetheless eligible for WIC when the wife was pregnant. Many Americans must combine work and social assistance because their job leaves them poor, or close to it.

One culprit is low pay. Consider the federal minimum wage, which Congress updates too infrequently to keep up with inflation. The current wage of $7.25 per hour would have to be $10.64 to equal the purchasing power of its 1968 peak.[4] Indeed, at $10.64, the minimum wage would approximate the "poverty-level wage"—what a full-time worker must earn to reach the poverty line for a family of four. One-fourth of male workers and one-third of female workers earn less than this amount.[5]

Yet other Americans toggle between work and work-plus-welfare as their incomes and situations fluctuate. Every year, one in seven earners experiences a drop in earnings of 50 percent or more, while one in five experiences a 25 percent drop.[6] During these troughs, individuals and families may fall into social assistance eligibility. The consensus among most researchers is that income volatility has increased over time, particularly for family earnings.[7]

The frequent combination of work and welfare is uniquely American. Single mothers in the United States, most of whom are separated, divorced, or widowed, both work more hours per week and experience far higher poverty rates than their counterparts in other rich industrialized countries.[8] Poverty among workers is higher in the United States partly because the minimum wage is not only lower than in the past but also lower than in other economically advanced nations. It came to only 38 percent of the country's median wage in 2011, the second-lowest ratio among twenty-five rich nations (the ratio was 45 percent in Canada, 54 percent in Australia, and 60 percent in France).[9]

High levels of poverty and near poverty among both nonworkers and workers, along with considerable volatility in incomes, result in widespread use of means-tested programs. Dave and Marcella's need for support is less of an exception than it may seem—the social assistance component of the American welfare state is hardly the small and residual tier that many believe it to be. Instead, it's a large and crucial set of programs that will at one time or another touch most American lives.

SOCIAL ASSISTANCE PROGRAMS FOR
THE POOR: LIFE IN THE BOTTOM TIER

Given how tightly targeted these means-tested programs typically are, their widespread use underscores just how little income many Americans have. The United States does offer help with life's necessities for those in and near poverty: food, shelter, cash, health insurance.[10] But most of these programs require would-be recipients to have very low income and asset levels in order to qualify. Benefit levels are meager. The programs are also heavily stigmatized, so many of the eligible don't even sign up. Some of the programs are wait-listed and can't cover all the eligible. The end result is that most programs for the poor leave recipients in poverty; taken together, American antipoverty programs don't do much to relieve poverty, especially compared with what other rich nations are able to achieve.

Our family's initial confusion about Marcella's eligibility—not to mention the revelation two years later that she was in a different Medi-Cal program than we had thought—shows that the rules for enrolling in means-tested programs are incredibly complex and confusing.[11] They vary substantially by program and by state, leading to uneven coverage. Usually, recipients must have incomes at or below the federal poverty level, but some programs in some states reach into the ranks of the working poor and even the lower middle class. For example, pregnant women with incomes up to 200 or 250 percent of the poverty line may be eligible for Medicaid, and children whose families have incomes up to 300 percent of the FPL ($69,150 for a family of four in 2012)[12] may be eligible for the Children's Health Insurance Program (up to 400 percent of the FPL in New York, the most generous state).[13] As Dave and Marcella learned with Medicaid, some programs and states additionally require that participants have assets below a certain level. Several programs have categorical criteria as well, such as being poor *and* either aged, blind, or disabled for SSI, or being poor *and* a pregnant or postpartum woman or a child under the age of five deemed at "nutritional risk" for WIC.

Due to these varying eligibility criteria, a given individual or family may qualify for some means-tested programs but not for others, and must apply for each separately (although some are linked). When Dave had to confirm the value of his Datsun pickup for the Medi-Cal asset test, the process was straightforward: because Medi-Cal is a state agency, it could look at the Department of Motor Vehicles' database to determine the value (it took Dave's purchase price and applied depreciation). Separately, Dave had to confirm the pickup's value with SSI, a much more complicated and time-consuming process. SSI is run by the federal Social Security Administration, which could see the value that Medi-Cal was using for the pickup, but wouldn't adopt it. Instead, the agency made Dave get an affidavit from a mechanic attesting to the pickup's value. He had to leave Marcella's bedside at the rehab hospital and travel back up to Redding to do so.

Because eligibility for means-tested programs is based on criteria like income that could change, recipients typically have to reapply periodically and prove again that they qualify for the assistance. Marcella has to provide Dave's paycheck stubs and other information for each of the programs in which she is enrolled, at intervals that vary from annually to every three months. People can drift in and out of programs, either because their incomes or other factors change, or because they fail to reapply. This "churning" creates real problems, especially in the health insurance programs, where breaks in coverage can mean going without needed care or prescription medicines.[14] At one point, Marcella and Dave found out that Logan was no longer listed in the system as having health insurance. We don't know why; the termination code was #99, the catchall code, so all we know is that he wasn't terminated for reasons 1 through 98.

Despite their neediness, many people who are eligible for means-tested programs don't enroll. "Take-up" rates are very low. Over 60 percent of American children who lack health insurance are eligible for Medicaid or CHIP but aren't enrolled.[15] Only 72 percent of those eligible for food stamps are enrolled (and only 34 percent of eligible senior citizens are). Complicated application procedures and confusing eligibility criteria are one barrier: many only seek information about these programs and fight their way in when they're truly desperate, like Dave and Marcella. Outreach efforts are often modest in scope (and vary by state and by program). And the enduring stigma surrounding means-tested programs reduces take-up rates as well. When I mentioned to Dave that California is the only state that does not allow SSI recipients to receive food stamps (see chapter 5)— suggesting that Marcella could get food stamps anywhere else—he blanched. He too drew a line: food stamps are just too demeaning. Attitudes among recipients reflect attitudes among the public; surveys reveal high levels of stigma around means-tested programs. Views are more negative toward programs whose recipients are thought to be responsible for their situations (such as Aid to Families with Dependent Children/TANF for poor single mothers) and less severe for programs whose beneficiaries are perceived as less blameworthy for their plight (such as Medicaid, because everyone needs medical care at some point, and school lunch programs, because children can't be blamed for their family's poverty).[16]

Partly because of public antipathy, many means-tested programs have withered on the vine. "Welfare," or AFDC/TANF cash assistance to poor families with children, has always been the least popular social assistance program, and was completely hollowed out by its 1996 reform. It now benefits only a fraction of the nation's poor families. Originally, the program was meant to keep poor mothers at home with their children, and federal spending covered as many recipients as states deemed eligible. The 1996 reform imposed a work requirement on recipient adults—overturning the program's original intent—and a five-year lifetime limit on benefits.[17] It also capped federal funding at preform levels, a "block grant" for each state that falls in real value over time.[18] As a result of these changes, welfare is now a very small program, costing the federal government less than 4 percent of what it spends on Social Security (see figure 3.1). The number of recipients shrank from 13 million in 1996 to 4 million in 2011.[19] In

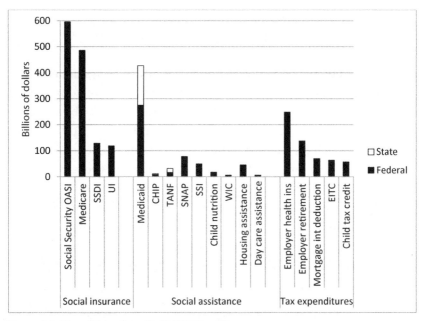

Figure 3.1 Size of American Social Welfare Programs

Note: 2011 amounts, except federal tax expenditures, which are from 2013, and state Earned Income Tax Credits, which are from 2008. Black portion of bar denotes federal spending; white portion is state spending. There is a state component for Medicaid, CHIP, TANF, child nutrition, day care assistance, and state EITCs, but for some of these programs state spending is so small that it is barely visible on the figure. The Unemployment Insurance figure is for federal and state spending combined; because of the Great Recession, total spending is higher than normal and includes a greater federal share due to emergency benefits.

Sources: Center on Budget and Policy Priorities, "Policy Basics: Introduction to SNAP," July 9, 2012; CBPP, "Chartbook: SNAP Helps Struggling Families Put Food on the Table," July 9, 2012, http://www.cbpp.org/cms/index.cfm?fa=view&id=3744; CBPP, "Policy Basics: Where Do Our Federal Tax Dollars Go?," August 13, 2012; CBPP, "Policy Basics: An Introduction to TANF," December 4, 2012; Office of Management and Budget, FY2013 Budget Historical Tables, table 11.3, "Outlays for Payments for Individuals by Category and Major Program: 1940–2017," http://www.whitehouse.gov/omb/budget/Historicals/; Congressional Budget Office, "Distribution of Major Tax Expenditures in the Individual Income Tax System," and Kaiser Family Foundation, "Total Medicaid Spending," http://kff.org/medicaid/state-indicator/total-medicaid-spending-fy2010/; Georgetown University Health Policy Institute, "Federal and State Share of CHIP Spending, FY2011," http://www.dev.mdvinteractive.com/ccf/wp-content/uploads/2012/04/CHIP-Spending.pdf; National Conference of State Legislatures, Early Care and Education State Budget Actions FY 2011, http://www.ncsl.org/Portals/1/Documents/cyf/2011EARLYCAREBUDGETREPORT.pdf; CBPP, "A Hand Up: How State Earned Income Tax Credits Help Working Families Escape Poverty in 2011," http://www.cbpp.org/files/4-18-11sfp.pdf.

1973, the program covered 80 percent of poor children; now it covers only 21 percent.[20] In other words, most poor children once received welfare. Now most do not.[21]

Federal housing assistance has also gone by the wayside. From the 1930s to the mid-1990s, this aid mostly supported public housing projects. Since then, the government has been destroying public housing stock and encouraging people to use rental vouchers for private-market apartments instead.[22] Now five times as many households (10 million people) live in private apartments subsidized by these "Section 8" vouchers as live in public housing projects. However, millions more are on waiting lists for the vouchers.[23]

Other means-tested programs have been allowed to grow, although that expansion is now threatened. During the 1990s, states received latitude to experiment with the use of Medicaid funds, often extending coverage to new groups. Governors and public hospitals pushed hard for this expansion to secure federal reimbursement for what would otherwise be free care.[24] And the expansion had support from both sides of the political aisle: liberals viewed Medicaid growth as a way to protect poor children in the absence of universal health insurance, and some Republicans and business groups advocated the expansion as a way to forestall demand for national health insurance.[25] In 2011, 55.7 million people were enrolled in Medicaid, up from 23 million in 1990 and 34.5 million in 2000; over 70 million, or one in five Americans, were enrolled for at least one month during 2011.[26] Now Medicaid is one of the largest items in the federal budget, along with Social Security, Medicare, and defense, and second only to education as the largest budget item for states. However, its further growth is threatened. Governors in about half the states refused to participate in the Affordable Care Act's expansion of Medicaid to all poor people. And there are proposals to convert Medicaid's federal funding to a block grant, as in the TANF reform (see chapter 6).

The food stamp program has grown as well. With the decline of cash welfare, food stamps have become a central support for low-income Americans. The Supplemental Nutrition Assistance Program benefits far more people: 47 million in 2011 to TANF's 4 million. Over time, participation in SNAP has increased markedly, from 5 percent of the US population in 1972 to 14 percent in 2011.[27] The program's recent growth began during the George W. Bush administration due to broadened eligibility and more aggressive outreach efforts, and increased further during the Great Recession with heightened need. However, SNAP's expansion has invited attacks reminiscent of the longtime demonization of welfare. In May 2011, former House Speaker and short-lived Republican presidential candidate Newt Gingrich called Barack Obama "the most successful food stamp president in American history." Then benefit increases enacted during the Great Recession expired, and in 2013 the Republican-controlled House led efforts to reduce SNAP further and de-couple it from the farm bill, where food stamps had long coexisted with agricultural subsidies, backed by a bipartisan coalition of rural agricultural and urban interests.[28]

Unique among means-tested programs, SSI has grown without attack, probably because it benefits a very specific group (poor aged, blind, or disabled people like Marcella) and is far smaller than Medicaid or SNAP. Due to Supreme Court rulings and new statutes increasing eligibility, particularly among disabled children and nonelderly adults, SSI grew from 1.8 percent of the population in 1975 to 2.5 percent in 2011.[29]

You wouldn't know it from the political challenges, but spending and benefits in most means-tested programs remain quite low. Except for Medicaid, total spending is but a fraction of expenditures occurring in the upper tiers of the American welfare state, such as Social Security or the big social-purpose tax breaks (fig. 3.1). Low benefits are also the norm, because of the long-standing concern that overly generous means-tested benefits will foster dependency. Typical TANF and SSI cash benefits are much smaller than Social Security or Social Security Disability Insurance benefits and leave recipients well below the poverty line, even when combined with food stamps (fig. 3.2). While the federal poverty line for a single person in 2011 was $908, the average monthly SSI benefit for an aged person was $398; for a blind person, $520; and for a disabled person, $519.[30] Consider how

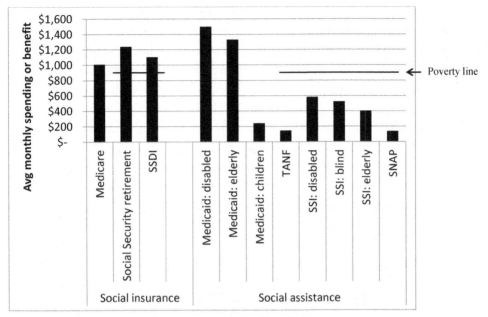

Figure 3.2 Benefit Levels in American Social Welfare Programs

Note: Figure shows average monthly spending or benefit per beneficiary. The single-person poverty line is drawn in for the cash programs. Medicaid spending is federal and state spending, averaged for each type of beneficiary. TANF benefit is from the median state. SSI benefits are federal (no state supplements), averaged across for each type of beneficiary. *Sources:* Medicare: *2012 Annual Report of the Boards of Trustees of the Federal Hospital Insurance and Federal Supplementary Medical Insurance Trust Funds,* 223. Social Security retirement and Survivors Insurance: http://www.ssa.gov/pressoffice/basicfact.htm. SSDI: Social Security Administration, Annual Statistical Supplement, 2012, table 5.D1. Medicaid: Amanda Cassidy, "Per Capita Caps in Medicaid," Health Policy Brief, *Health Affairs,* April 18, 2013. TANF: Ife Finch and Liz Schott, "TANF Benefits Fell Further in 2011 and Are Worth Much Less Than in 1996 in Most States," Center on Budget and Policy Priorities, November 21, 2011. SSI: Social Security Administration, Annual Statistical Supplement, 2012, table 7.A1. SNAP: Center on Budget and Policy Priorities, "Policy Basics: Introduction to the Supplemental Nutrition Assistance Program (SNAP)," November 20, 2012.

low these benefits are: for example, the disabled face a variety of additional living expenses and needs not covered by Medicaid or other social assistance programs. How are they supposed to live on $519 a month?[31] In contrast, the average monthly payment for SSDI recipients that same year was twice as high—$1,100.[32] That is, the same disabled person could get double the monthly cash income if she were a former worker with social insurance rather than a nonworker eligible only for social assistance (like Marcella). And these are average figures; because SSDI benefits are linked to a recipient's earnings, they can be even higher, as we'll see below. TANF benefits are even lower than SSI: $426 per month in the median state for a *family of three*. With cash assistance levels so meager, food stamps are now a significant benefit for many of the poor, with the average amount for a family of three in 2011 equaling $397, and for a single person $153.[33] It's tough to live on a food stamp budget, however: the SNAP assistance works out to $1.50 per meal per person. Only Medicaid provides a comprehensive benefit—but one that you have to impoverish yourself to get, as Dave and Marcella have learned.

As a result of tight eligibility requirements and low benefits, means-tested programs leave most poor people in the United States poor. Even when including the value of noncash benefits such as food stamps and housing vouchers, these programs don't budge poverty very much.[34] Outcomes are even worse in some states than others, as chapter 5 details. The failure of American social policy to alleviate poverty is especially apparent in international comparison. Consider poor single mothers, a group heavily stigmatized in the United States. American social programs move only 15 percent of them out of poverty, compared with 60 to 91 percent moved out of poverty in other economically advanced nations.[35] These cross-national differences in poverty outcomes don't stem from economic differences. The market economies of other rich nations produce poverty rates that are just as high as in the United States: 26 to 30 percent of the population earns less than 50 percent of the national median income in each of these countries. The difference lies in taxing and especially in social spending, which do far more to tackle poverty elsewhere. Including the value of taxes and social programs reduces the American poverty rate to 17 percent, but pushes poverty below 10 percent in many countries, and as low as 5 percent in Scandinavia.[36]

In sum, as Marcella and Dave have learned, the bottom tier of the American welfare state provides a safety net of a sort, but leaves most people in poverty, struggling to make ends meet.

SOCIAL INSURANCE PROGRAMS FOR
WORKERS: A MUCH BETTER TIER

The social policy tier Marcella had been trying to reach before the accident is the "upper" tier of social insurance programs for workers and their dependents. These programs include Social Security pensions for retirees and for the surviving spouses and children of deceased workers; SSDI for permanently disabled workers; Medicare health insurance for older and disabled Americans; Unemployment Insurance; and workers' compensation for injured jobholders. Most of these programs have more generous benefits than the means-tested tier. And their recipients suffer little stigma, because these are "insurance" programs funded mostly by earmarked contributions, not general tax revenues.[37] Nonetheless, even this tier, the highest public tier the United States offers, has its shortcomings compared with social protections in other rich nations. As chapter 6 details, benefits fall short of need, and coverage is for workers and dependents only, not all citizens.

Our mother's experience illustrates the desirable features of Social Security and Medicare, especially for retirees, compared with the means-tested programs in which Dave and Marcella are enrolled. As a retired worker, Mom enjoys the same monthly Social Security check and the same Medicare benefits no matter where she lives. Several years ago, she moved from high-cost California to low-cost northern Minnesota, safe in the knowledge that her income and health insurance would remain the same. In contrast, if Dave and Marcella contemplated moving, they would have to examine carefully the Medicaid benefits offered, which can vary dramatically from state to state, as chapter 5 details. As a Medicare recipient, Mom can see pretty much any physician she wishes, while Marcella has had a difficult time finding physicians who will take Medicaid.[38] Mom faces no stigma in drawing her Social Security pension or receiving her Medicare insurance. She will never have to reapply and re-prove eligibility, as Marcella does.[39]

While means-tested programs use caseworkers as gatekeepers to skeptically "test" applicants for eligibility, the Social Security system is set up to maximize recipients' benefits. When Mom first retired, she had the choice of a benefit based on her own work history or half the benefit based on our father's work history, which turned out to be higher (they were married long enough for her as a divorced spouse to use his earnings as her Social Security basis). After Dad passed away, her benefit increased to his full benefit, well above the poverty line.[40] In contrast, Marcella's SSI benefit leaves her below the poverty line, like most means-tested program recipients. Mom's extra retirement savings outside Social Security do not affect her Social Security pension (although at high income levels, retirees do pay taxes on their Social Security benefits). In contrast, neither Dave nor Marcella can earn much extra money without her SSI benefit being cut. Social Security has high benefits compared with the means-tested tier, and a take-up rate approaching 100 percent; also, its benefit formula gives proportionately higher benefits to those who earned less during their working years.[41] As a result, the senior poverty rate is under 9 percent, compared with nearly 22 percent among children.[42] It's the most effective antipoverty program in the United States.

Like other retired workers and their spouses, Mom has health insurance through Medicare. She is automatically enrolled in Part A, the hospital insurance portion funded by the Medicare payroll tax, which covers inpatient hospital care, skilled nursing care (as in a rehabilitation hospital), and hospice care. Like the vast majority of Medicare recipients, she also participates in the optional Part B portion, which covers doctors' visits and outpatient hospital care. For Part B she paid a monthly premium of $104.90 in 2013 (such premiums cover one-fourth of Part B expenses while general tax revenues cover the other three-fourths). In addition, she has a Part D prescription drug plan, an optional benefit that became available in 2006 for which she also pays a monthly premium (the drug program is funded by general tax revenues as well). Some seniors have enrolled in the Medicare Part C option, by which they get all their health care (Parts A, B, and D) covered together by a private managed care plan, such as a Medicare HMO.

Whereas Social Security is a nearly unparalleled policy success, bringing most seniors above the poverty line and making retirement a reality, Medicare is a more complicated case. When signed into law in 1965, it instantly transformed senior citizens from the age group least likely to have health insurance to the group most likely to. However, the basic package of program benefits didn't change for forty years, until the prescription drug option was added. Also, Medicare is incomplete insurance; it covers only about half of seniors' total medical costs. There is substantial "cost sharing" that Medicare enrollees pay out of pocket, including monthly Part B premiums, monthly prescription drug plan premiums, deductibles, and coinsurance, which can add up quickly. There are also big gaps in coverage. Medicare doesn't cover vision or dental exams or hearing aids, for example, which can be expensive: my colleague's stepmother had to pay $4,800 out of pocket for hers.[43] Most seniors have help in meeting these expenses, either because they are low income and also qualify for Medicaid, which pays their out-of-pocket costs for them; or because they have private insurance from a former employer or have purchased it individually ("medigap" policies); or because they have enrolled in a Medicare managed care plan that covers some of these expenses. All that said, the value of the Medicare benefits package has grown over time, as the program has given seniors access to advances in medicine. Concomitantly, real per-person spending has increased dramatically, largely because medical inflation exceeds ordinary inflation by a substantial margin.

Social Security and Medicare benefit not only retired workers but also permanently disabled workers who are eligible. To get SSDI cash benefits, a worker must have been employed and paid payroll taxes for enough total quarters, and recently enough, to be covered by the system (Marcella had not).[44] A physician must provide medical evidence of disability as well. Benefits are based on an individual's earnings history (intellectually disabled adults can get SSDI benefits based on a parent's Social Security contributions). Because SSDI is intended only for the permanently disabled, not for those who can return to work after a few weeks or months, there is a five-month waiting period before benefits begin.[45]

Medicare is available to the permanently disabled as well, but only after a 24-month waiting period (which is really a 29-month period from the onset of disability: 5 months until SSDI eligibility takes effect, then 24 additional months for Medicare). Policy makers instituted the waiting period in part to save money and in part to minimize the incentive for jobholders to seek a disability designation merely to get health insurance. Yet the waiting period for Medicare can cause considerable hardship—or worse—for the newly disabled. Randy Shepherd, a thirty-six-year-old Arizona plumber and father of three, has cardiomyopathy, a condition that severely weakened his heart. Doctors told him in 2010 that he needed a heart transplant to survive. Some marveled that he was still alive. Unable to work, Shepherd went on SSDI and awaited Medicare eligibility. In the meantime, he enrolled in Arizona's Medicaid program, the only insurance he could get because of his preexisting condition. The state Medicaid office authorized the transplant, but then reversed itself in October 2010, because the state legislature had eliminated funding for many transplants, including those for Shepherd's condition, due to a budget deficit. With no Medicaid coverage for the transplant, Shepherd and his family then had to hope he'd survive until his date of Medicare eligibility.[46] At least Shepherd had Medicaid: one-third of those in the SSDI Medicare waiting period have no insurance at all.[47] As for our family, even if Marcella had been eligible for Medicare, there's a real question as to what she would have done for insurance during the eligibility waiting period.

Unemployment Insurance and workers' compensation are forms of social insurance too, though far less universal than Social Security and Medicare. After Dave's paid family leave ran out following the accident, his boss laid him off so he could get UI (business was slow anyway, and there wasn't any work for him). Dave was lucky to qualify—most Americans don't. Even though UI is funded by state and federal payroll taxes on employers, a worker must meet the state's requirements for wages earned or time worked during a certain "base period," and the job loss must be involuntary (you don't qualify if you quit, were dismissed for misconduct, or were unable or unavailable to work). Part-time, temporary, and self-employed workers—a substantial proportion of the US workforce—do not qualify for UI at all. Outside of recessions, fewer than half the unemployed workers have received UI benefits during the last twenty-five years, and the proportion of workers eligible has shrunk over time.[48]

The final type of social insurance is workers' compensation, a program meant to provide partial wage replacement and medical benefits for those injured on the job (in exchange for which the worker can't sue his or her employer). It is a form of social insurance, although less public and more private than the programs just mentioned. The program is mostly state run, and states either require employers to pay into a public fund or allow them to purchase private insurance or to self-insure. As with UI, benefits vary substantially across states.[49]

To summarize, workers are protected by several forms of social insurance that help cushion income loss from retirement, permanent disability, or short-term injury, and provide health insurance in old age. Although UI and workers' compensation fail to cover many American workers and provide only modest benefits, Social Security and Medicare are traditionally viewed as universal, generous programs that substantially help their recipients. They are restricted to eligible workers, however, and can't help those like Marcella who haven't worked enough.

THE PRIVATE WELFARE SYSTEM OF EMPLOYER-PROVIDED BENEFITS: THE MOST DESIRABLE TIER

The top tier, the one that Marcella and Dave had hoped to reach with her new nursing career, is the private welfare system of employer-provided benefits. For example, through my employer I get a variety of "fringe benefits," including health insurance, dental insurance, a retirement plan, group life insurance, short-term disability insurance, paid vacation, paid sick days, and paid maternity and parental leave.[50] Dave gets none of these. In retirement he'll only have Social Security, not a private pension or 401(k) savings like me. When he is sick or takes vacation time to be a counselor at the YMCA camp near town, he doesn't get paid, whereas I would. And of course, he didn't have health insurance before Marcella's accident. Offering such benefits is not required of employers. They have some incentives to do so—for example, employers aren't taxed on the contributions they make toward employees' health insurance or pensions. However, offering such benefits is still costly and may not make economic sense for certain employers, especially smaller firms and those employing lower-wage workers (my family's health insurance costs about 30 percent more than a full-time minimum-wage worker earns in a year).

Consequently, the private welfare system's chief shortcoming is that it isn't available to everyone. Nonworkers are by definition shut out of it. Moreover, the employer decides whether workers (and their dependents) will be covered. In 2009, just two-thirds of workers aged eighteen to sixty-four had employer-provided health insurance; just half such workers had an employer that sponsored a retirement plan.[51] Furthermore, access to employer-provided benefits is highly skewed by income. Such benefits are most widely available to the middle class and especially the affluent in higher-paid jobs. If you sort US firms by the average wage they pay, most firms in the top quartile offer retirement benefits and paid sick leave, compared with only one-third of the firms in the bottom quartile.[52]

An additional concern with this private welfare system is that it creates labor market rigidity. People may be reluctant to change jobs or to start their own company for fear of losing their benefits, a form of "job lock" that undermines economic dynamism.

More crucially, the employer-provided system is eroding. The proportion of working-age Americans with employer-provided health insurance is falling.[53] For those with insurance, coverage is deteriorating, with fewer covered services, tighter physician and hospital networks, and greater out-of-pocket costs.[54] Retirement plans are changing in a way that creates greater uncertainty about retirement income: most firms have moved away from traditional "defined benefit" pension plans, which promise a specific benefit in retirement, toward "defined contribution" plans such as 401(k)s. These promise only that a specific contribution is made toward retirement; the size of the retirement benefit is unknown, and depends on the performance of investments.[55] Such changes place more risk on workers.

THE TAX EXPENDITURE SYSTEM:
THE ICING ON THE CAKE (FOR SOME)

As if it weren't bad enough that more affluent people like me tend to get more employer-provided benefits than folks like Dave and Marcella, the tax expenditure system exacerbates the situation. Many social protections in the United States are provided less by direct-spending programs than by the series of tax breaks, credits, and deferrals known as the tax expenditure system. For example, the United States doesn't have national health insurance (nor is the Affordable Care Act national health insurance covering everyone; see chapter 6), but it does subsidize employer-provided health insurance by exempting the premiums paid by the employer and employee from taxation. Few Americans receive public housing assistance, but many more enjoy the subsidization of home ownership: mortgage interest is exempt from taxation for those who itemize their deductions when filing their income tax. The United States doesn't have family allowances or universal public day care or preschool, but does have a Child Tax Credit and child-care tax credit to subsidize the cost of raising children. The United States has a low minimum wage and a high share of working poor in international comparison, but it also has an Earned Income Tax Credit that shores up the incomes of low-wage workers (especially those with children) by refunding part or all of the federal income and payroll taxes they pay. Through the tax expenditure system, the government provides social benefits—not through spending directly, but by foregoing revenue through these tax credits and deductions.[56]

The problem with the tax expenditure system is that it's huge—lost revenues total $1.1 trillion per year, more than the sum raised by the individual income tax[57]—and the affluent benefit the most, getting the most breaks and saving the most on their taxes.[58] For example, my husband and I itemize our deductions and so get a break for home mortgage interest, state and local taxes, and charitable contributions. We lower our taxes still further by using tax-free flexible spending accounts to offset out-of-pocket medical costs and, when the kids were younger, dependent care expenses. The amount we contribute to our employer-provided health insurance and retirement plans isn't taxed to begin with. These tax breaks save us, and cost the US Treasury, thousands of dollars a year.

In contrast, Dave and Marcella can't benefit from many of these breaks. They do itemize deductions on their tax form—only 30 percent of taxpayers do[59]—and so they can take deductions for home mortgage interest, state and local taxes, and charitable contributions. However, because Dave's company doesn't offer benefits, they don't get any of the high-value deductions for employer-provided benefits like health insurance, a retirement plan, or a flexible spending account. Given Medi-Cal's income restrictions after the accident, Dave and Marcella can't afford child care, so they won't take the child-care tax credit. The only breaks they can take that my husband and I can't are the Earned Income Tax Credit and the Child Tax Credit.

In sum, the American welfare state offers vastly different levels of protections to people in its different tiers. Just how different becomes evident when calamity strikes.

YOUR FATE DEPENDS ON YOUR TIER

If my brother or I had been in that car that bright February morning, we would have fared very differently from Marcella in the coverage we would have received.

Marcella: The Public Lower Tier for Nonworkers

As we have already seen, Marcella is relegated to the lowest tier of the welfare state because she is a nonworker. She hadn't worked enough quarters at the bank before returning to school to qualify for the social insurance programs for the disabled (SSDI and Medicare). As a result, she must rely on SSI for income and Medicaid (Medi-Cal) for health insurance. SSI provides smaller cash benefits than SSDI (less than the poverty rate for a single person), and while Medicaid provides fairly comprehensive health coverage, there are limitations—the refusal of many doctors to accept Medicaid patients, and restrictions on benefits such as monthly prescriptions, to name two. And of course, to remain eligible for these means-tested programs, Marcella's income and assets must continue to be below the Medicaid thresholds in her state, with all the injurious consequences discussed in chapter 2—for example, not being able to accept financial help from relatives. She does have access to thirteen hours per day of state-funded personal care assistance, a benefit linked to her Medi-Cal eligibility. Yet if she were unmarried, she would probably be living in poverty, as many of the disabled do.[60] As it is, she and Dave have to keep their income below the modest living standard budget in order to retain her Medi-Cal.

Dave: The Public Upper Tier for Workers

Dave would experience a different tier of the American welfare state if he were the one injured on that fateful day. Let us imagine for a moment that he is single. He has worked steadily for two decades and has accrued more than enough quarters of work to be an insured worker. If Dave were to be permanently disabled, he would qualify for SSDI, in his case a monthly payment of $1,267. However, it wouldn't start until five months after his disability began.[61]

In the short term, Dave would be lucky that he lived in California, one of five states with short-term disability insurance. This cash assistance program is funded through a payroll tax, and would pay weekly benefits equivalent to about 55 percent of his usual wage for up to one year.[62] These payments could tide him over until SSDI kicked in.

Two years after SSDI eligibility, Dave would qualify for Medicare. There's the question of what he'd do for health insurance for the intervening twenty-nine months. He has no employer-provided health insurance to extend through the Consolidated Omnibus Budget Reconciliation Act (popularly known as COBRA, which lasts only eighteen months anyway).[63] He'd probably have to enroll in Medi-Cal, as much as he would hate to liquidate and spend down his assets to do so. Since the insurance exchanges of the Affordable Care Act came into effect in January 2014, he could buy insurance there without having to meet an asset test (see chapter 6). However, these private insurance plans wouldn't cover all the needs of a severely disabled person, particularly personal care assistance.

For that matter, neither would Medicare, when Dave would finally be eligible. As health insurance, Medicare has a lot of holes: huge deductibles, copays, and monthly premiums, including 20 percent coinsurance on incontinence supplies and medical equipment. A disabled beneficiary's share could run thousands of dollars a year. Yet in most states, Dave would be banned from buying a private medigap plan to cover this cost sharing.

As long-term care insurance, Medicare is even worse. It doesn't cover personal care assistance at all. Dave could pay for that help out of pocket, and as long as he stayed out of any means-tested programs, family members could help him financially with the expense of hiring personal care professionals. But personal care assistants are extremely expensive; he would quickly exhaust his own resources and the ability of family members to help. In the end, he would probably have to spend down to Medi-Cal eligibility in order to get the long-term services and supports he would need as a disabled person.

Nonetheless, a worker is better off than a nonworker in several regards. Social insurance benefits—at least the cash benefits—are greater than those of the social assistance tier. The lack of income and asset requirements means that recipients can use their own resources and accept financial help from relatives without endangering their eligibility for public benefits. However, the bottom line is still dismal. The absence of a social insurance program for long-term care means that a disabled worker would probably need to spend down to Medicaid eligibility to get the personal care he or she needs, just as thousands of middle-class older Americans in need of nursing home care do every year.[64]

Andrea: The Advantages of the Private Welfare System

If my car were run off the road and I were left permanently disabled, I'd have a completely different experience from either Marcella or Dave, although I too would ultimately struggle to pay for personal care assistants.

As an insured worker who has paid into Social Security and Medicare, I would qualify for SSDI payments of around $2,600 per month after five months and then Medicare after twenty-four more months, like Dave. Note that my SSDI benefits would be greater than Dave's, because my salary is higher—even though our level of disability would be the same.

On top of the public programs, however, I have access to a set of private welfare benefits from my employer. I am fortunate enough to teach at MIT, which offers a particularly generous set of benefits, beginning with long-term disability insurance. I would be paid 60 percent of my previous salary for the entire time I was disabled, with the monthly payments reduced by the amount I received from SSDI once those payments began after the five-month waiting period. MIT would also continue to pay the full cost of my MIT health, dental, and vision plans and my group life insurance, and would continue to make contributions to my retirement savings. These benefits would continue until I reached the "normal" Social Security retirement age of sixty-seven for my cohort (people born after 1960). As it happens, I also have been paying into a supplemental disability plan that I joined at a group rate at a previous employer. This plan would pay $864 per month on top of my MIT long-term disability.

In my case, then, the private and upper-tier public welfare state would weave together to provide quite substantial benefits. My income would be 60 percent of my pre-accident income (SSDI + my employer's long-term disability plan) plus the $864 from my supplemental disability plan. For health insurance, I'd be covered by my employer's plan for the first twenty-nine months, and then by my employer's plan with Medicare as secondary payer thereafter.[65] I would therefore be protected from Medicare's substantial out-of-pocket costs, to which Dave, lacking employer-provided insurance, would be exposed. I'd also have dental and vision coverage, which Medicare wouldn't provide Dave (we're both nearsighted). I'd have no interruptions in income or health insurance and could retain my assets, unlike Marcella in the means-tested tier—indeed, my retirement assets would grow, as my employer would continue to pay into my pension account. As long as I stayed out of means-tested programs, my husband could continue to work without affecting my eligibility.

When I reached retirement age, the Social Security Administration would automatically switch my SSDI benefits to Social Security retirement benefits (this would happen for Dave as well when he reached the age of 67). I would also receive income from my employer-provided retirement funds. My primary health insurance would be Medicare, with MIT paying 70 percent of the cost of a medigap supplemental policy, which would cover the Medicare out-of-pocket costs. Although the disabled under 65 years old cannot buy medigap plans, once a disabled person is 65, she may buy one—because now the risk pool is not just the disabled but all those over the age of 65, only some of whom will turn out to need expensive health care.

The big issue for me would be paying personal care assistants. My rosy financial picture as a socially insured worker with generous employer-provided benefits disintegrates when it comes to my long-term care needs. There is no social insurance LTC program, and my income would be too high for Medicaid, the only public source of long-term services and supports. I would need to pay for personal care assistants out of pocket both before and after the age of 65. Twelve hours of care per day, at $20 per hour, would total $87,600 per year. Even at $12 per hour—the lowest rate I could find in Massachusetts—the annual bill would come to $52,560. And the bill could be much higher: a bioethics professor in New York whose husband is paralyzed from the shoulders down spends nearly $250,000 per year for his twenty-four-hour-per-day personal care.[66]

There is private LTC insurance, which I could buy (although not after I became disabled), but it's a highly flawed market. The coverage is expensive, and yet the benefits are time limited and often meager. Their payout depends on the financial strength of the insurer, which may be questionable for a policy purchased years earlier (a decade ago, one hundred insurers offered private LTC insurance; now only a dozen actively do).[67] As a result, very few people purchase private LTC insurance, and usually not until their midfifties or later, leaving them uncovered if they become disabled earlier in life. Even if a person did have private LTC insurance, it would be of little help in the face of a lifelong disability: such policies typically have benefit periods of three to five years, not the decades the nonelderly disabled need. With the short reach of private LTC insurance and the absence of social insurance, Medicaid is the default for most.

The experiences of Michael Ogg illustrate the near inevitability of Medicaid for those who need long-term services and supports (LTSS). Dr. Ogg is a fifty-eight-year-old physics professor with a progressive form of multiple sclerosis that forced his retirement and left him functionally quadriplegic, unable to perform the activities of daily living. Fortuitously, he has private LTC insurance through a former employer. By carefully utilizing just a few personal care hours each day, he has been able to remain in his home, which he renovated for wheelchair accessibility using $150,000 of his own funds, as no public funds cover this necessary work. However, he is about to run into the lifetime cap on benefits. Dr. Ogg is now trying to move his remaining assets into a special-needs trust so he can qualify for Medicaid by the time his private LTC insurance runs out. It's a race against time: if his private insurance terminates before he can get on Medicaid, he'll have to pay for personal care out of pocket, which will quickly deplete the last of his resources. This will make it hard for him to support his two teenage daughters (his marriage ended after his diagnosis), and likely force him into a nursing home, as he'd have no other way to pay for personal care assistance. Dr. Ogg writes, "Even for those with the option and ability to afford private LTC insurance, there is no private insurance that I am aware of that would provide the necessary level of support. The costs of LTSS are so high that very few people can afford it on their own. This leaves people like me with the following choices: bankruptcy, nursing home, or both."[68]

The question for me is how long my assets and income could manage to keep pace with my long-term support needs (after paying for a wheelchair van and home renovations or a new place to live). I could avoid Medicaid for a while, and I'd be better off than either Dave or Marcella as a result, able to avoid poverty and to accept help from my husband and relatives without penalty. Eventually, however, the expense of my needs would probably exhaust our assets and income, unless my husband could find a much more lucrative job—assuming he'd want to stick around at all: "diagnose and adios" is pretty frequent in this world, one disability expert told me. In the end, there's a good chance I would have to spend down to poverty and Medicaid eligibility even as a relatively affluent, privileged worker covered by both social insurance and extensive employer-provided benefits.

In sum, for workers wrapped in the protections offered by the public social insurance tier and by the private welfare system, an accident doesn't have to mean impoverishment, as it does for noncovered workers like Marcella. Or at least not right away: the lack of a social insurance LTC program means Medicaid in the end for most. There are many types and severities of disability, some of which are addressed more effectively by the system (such as the needs of cognitively impaired adults who qualify for SSDI and Medicare through their parents' work histories).[69] But for those like Marcella and Michael Ogg who need long-term services, the American system fails dramatically. In the United States, the shortcomings of the welfare state mean that disability spells poverty for many.

LESSONS FROM THE BOTTOM OF THE RABBIT HOLE

As our family has learned since Marcella's accident, woe to those who find themselves on the wrong side of the often arbitrary divisions of the American welfare state. How you are treated in times of need and what kinds of help you can expect to receive depend almost entirely on your status as a worker—and not only whether you are employed but for how long and for which employer. Workers who have worked long enough have access to the upper, more generous tier of social insurance programs. Some jobholders additionally enjoy private welfare benefits, although that depends entirely on the inclination of the employer. In contrast, nonworkers must make do with the lower tier of social assistance, with its often meager benefits and severe eligibility standards. The lower tier can be relatively generous—Medicaid offers fairly comprehensive insurance, if you can find a health care provider to accept it, and it can provide a fair amount of home health care, depending on the state. But it always exacts a profound price: financial strictures that reshape the recipient's life chances. And the holes in the American welfare state can leave even workers without protections from some of life's most serious risks.

Although much of this discussion concerns the systematic ways in which different groups get channeled into the different tiers of social policy, it's striking—and a little scary—how easily the same person could end up in one tier rather than another, depending on life circumstances. Political scientist Joe Soss writes,

> Consider the case of a working-class woman married to a man who serves as the family's sole breadwinner. If the man "disappears" by abandoning the woman and her children, she will likely be channeled into the AFDC/TANF program, with its meager benefits and harsh terms of participation. Alternatively, if the man "disappears" by dying, she and her children will likely be channeled into the [Social Security] Survivor's Insurance program [in the superior insurance tier of the system].[70]

Or consider my brother and me. We grew up in the same family, and yet circumstances thrust us into different welfare systems with wildly different benefits—even before the accident, let alone after.

What's scarier still? How hard it is to escape means-tested programs once you are in them, as the next chapter shows.

HOW MEANS-TESTED PROGRAMS KEEP PEOPLE POOR

Means-tested programs for the poor have features that seem illogical, even cruel, from the perspective of helping these people and lifting them out of poverty. Benefit levels so low that recipients can't make ends meet. Bureaucratic hurdles and stigma that minimize enrollment. Asset ceilings that prohibit savings. Why would social assistance programs be designed like this?

These features make more sense when you consider the intent behind means-tested programs in the United States, and how these programs fit together with jobs and other social supports.[1] American means-tested programs aren't principally about pulling people out of poverty. Instead, they're intended to provide a safety net that is absolutely minimal (given its taxpayer funding), goes to the "deserving" rather than the undeserving, and doesn't deter holding a job. To achieve these goals, means-tested programs are tightly targeted on those at the very bottom of the socioeconomic ladder, with low income and asset ceilings.

Tight targeting addresses the main fear, which has always been that programs for the poor deter working. Thus from its inception, American social assistance was organized around the principle of "less eligibility" that originated in the British poor laws of the nineteenth century.[2] The idea back then was to deter paupers from workhouses by making conditions there worse than the worst job on the outside. In contemporary America, this idea persists: means-tested programs have to remain inferior to the alternative—the worst jobs at the worst wages. If benefits were easy to get, stigma free, and generous, it would be too hard to find people willing to take bottom-of-the-barrel jobs. There would be pressure on low-wage employers to improve pay and benefits. Instead, policy makers try to make means-tested programs as miserable as possible to discourage would-be applicants, minimize enrollment, and incentivize work in low-level jobs. And as conditions in the low-end job market have deteriorated over time, with shrinking real wages, an increase in part-time work, and the near disappearance of employer-provided benefits, means-tested programs have gotten worse in tandem.

The problem is that narrow targeting and fear of replacing work have perverse consequences: the programs' corresponding design features also prevent people from *leaving* poverty. The extreme eligibility criteria that tight targeting requires—the low income and asset ceilings—mean that as people leave assistance for work, their benefits first diminish and then disappear altogether. The cost of working is steep indeed, as the recipient loses cash assistance, housing, food assistance, child care subsidy, and medical insurance, one after another.

And there's little on the outside to replace these lost benefits. The high price of leaving assistance for work is not the fault of means-tested programs alone. Low-wage jobs don't provide child care or health insurance. They don't pay enough to cover market-rate rents or provide an adequate diet. There aren't other social programs to bridge the gap once the worker no longer qualifies for the means-tested ones. That social assistance traps people in poverty is an indictment, not just of that bottom tier of the American welfare state, but of the entire system.

THE BENEFITS LIMBO: HOW LOW CAN THEY GO?

The list of assistance program design features that help keep people poor begins with low benefit levels. Benefits must be kept from rising above the worst wages in the market. If these wages are low enough to produce a stratum of "working poor," then means-tested benefits must be set even lower, low enough to keep people in poverty. That antipoverty programs would keep people in poverty makes no sense—until you think about the programs in relation to the job market.

This dynamic is most evident in the cash assistance programs.

Consider Temporary Assistance for Needy Families: in no state do welfare benefits come close to lifting recipient families out of poverty. In the most generous TANF state, New York, the maximum benefit is less than half the federal poverty level. In the least generous state, Mississippi, the maximum TANF benefit is 11 percent of the poverty level. For a family of three, that's $2,040 for a *year*—a little more than the annual household income in Nigeria.[3] Adding the value of Supplemental Nutrition Assistance Program benefits fails to bring families above the poverty line, even in the most generous states.[4] Even SSI, which goes to the more sympathetic poor elderly, blind, and disabled populations, has below-poverty benefits.[5]

As the logic of less eligibility would dictate, means-tested benefits have deteriorated as conditions in the low-end job market have worsened. With Congress letting the minimum wage fall behind the rate of inflation, cash benefits have also fallen in real terms: the real value of both the minimum wage and the Aid to Families with Dependent Children and TANF benefits peaked in the late 1960s-early 1970s and has fallen since.[6]

The availability of means-tested programs has been curtailed as well. TANF programs have waiting lists in many states, as do child-care subsidy programs.[7] The Low-Income Home Energy Assistance Program for heating assistance typically runs out of money during the winter.[8] Only one in four low-income households receives rental subsidization,[9] and waiting lists for affordable housing are enormous. When Chicago opened its public housing waiting list in 2010 after demolishing 20,000 such units over the previous two decades, 200,000 families applied—more than the total number of households in Milwaukee, St. Louis, or Minneapolis.[10] In New York City, where 5,000 to 6,000 Housing Authority apartments become available each year, it would take thirty-eight years to get through the quarter-million-household waiting list.[11]

THE PARTICULAR SADNESS OF ASSET TESTS

Worse yet are asset limits. Even if poor people could save money on their modest incomes, they are prohibited from doing so.

Or if they are lucky enough to receive a little inheritance they might put away for the future, or save for a child, it has to disappear, fast. Most means-tested programs in most states have an asset test, which requires that an applicant not only be cash poor but also possess very minimal assets to qualify for assistance. Most of these asset test amounts haven't been raised in years, making the poor even worse off. As the Suze Ormans and Dave Ramseys of the world attest, the first step to financial stability is having an emergency fund, followed by saving for other needs: your next car, retirement, college. But most social assistance programs prohibit such savings, forcing the poor to stay poor. Without savings, not only can you not get ahead, but you can easily fall further behind.

This asset policy makes more sense when you consider its real purpose: not poverty reduction, but making sure that only the neediest and most deserving enroll in these assistance programs. The asset limits are intended to ensure that no one with a fat bank account is receiving aid. They are part of the effort to tightly target these programs, in other words.

But once people are in these programs, asset limits become a straitjacket.[12] It's very expensive to be poor, as Barbara Ehrenreich has documented so compellingly in her book *Nickel and Dimed*.[13] For one thing, if you can't save up for things you need, you end up paying top dollar. For example, low-income people often lack bank accounts and so lose precious dollars in fees to storefront check-cashing operations. They rent furniture and end up paying for each piece many times over. Or consider Ehrenreich's fellow waitress at a Florida family-style restaurant. She lived in a nearby hotel, paying an expensive nightly rate, because she didn't have a car or first and last months' rent to put down as a deposit for an apartment—and no hope of ever accruing such a sum at the low wages she was earning. As Anthony Wright of the consumer advocacy coalition Health Access California points out, "In our social policy, we encourage even poor families to have three months' rent in the bank, even [as] we threaten to take away their health care if they do."[14]

The ramifications of the asset test became apparent to my family one afternoon when a drunk driver hit Marcella's van as her sister was driving her back from physical therapy. Fortunately, there wasn't a lot of damage. But if there had been, Dave and Marcella would have been in trouble: how could they pay for an expensive repair? They face a real conundrum under Medi-Cal's dual income and asset restrictions. When purchasing home or auto insurance, people have to decide between a lower monthly premium with a higher deductible or a higher monthly premium paired with a lower deductible. Their choice depends on whether it's their income or their assets that are higher: those with greater savings but less income would choose a higher deductible and a lower monthly premium, while those with fewer assets but greater income would choose to pay more each month in exchange for a lower deductible. But what if *both* their income and their assets are low, as is the case with my brother and sister-in-law?

And then Dave and Marcella did face a crisis: the mechanism for the van's wheelchair ramp stopped working. The parts and labor needed to replace the motor and make some other repairs came to $3,000. Of course, they're not supposed to have $3,000 in cash, given the asset test. Fortuitously, their tax refund had just come in, and went straight back out to pay for the repair.

The other dilemma Dave faced was having a vehicle to transport the baby. When Marcella was being driven by a friend or family member in the van, he didn't have a way to drive Logan, because his pickup lacks a backseat (where state law stipulates that the infant car seat must be secured). For a while he used Mom's car, but she'd eventually need to return to Minnesota, taking her car with her. Dave worked desperately to get a 1968 Volkswagen Squareback up and running—selected, like the Datsun pickup, for its low value. Try as he might, to his enormous frustration he couldn't get it working, and the clock was ticking down. I had a brilliant idea: maybe Dave could lease a car. I see advertisements all the time that offer small sedans for $79 per month. That would be perfect: inexpensive, and leased rather than owned, so it wouldn't count against Dave and Marcella's asset limit. Ah, but there's the rub: the asset test. Leases require down payments of around $3,000. That's Dave and Marcella's entire asset limit. If

Dave were to lease a car, a social worker would ask: where did he get the money for the down payment?

Some states have made changes to their asset rules. Twenty-four have eliminated their asset tests for Medicaid, partly for administrative simplicity and cost savings: it's cheaper simply to cover poor people than to hound them about their assets and then deny care.[15] Forty-seven states have eliminated their asset test for the Children's Health Insurance Program. And in order to promote personal savings and greater financial security, President Obama's fiscal 2011 budget proposed raising asset tests for federally funded means-tested programs such as TANF, food stamps, and the Low-Income Home Energy Assistance Program to a minimum of $10,000. But in the polarized Congress this proposal went nowhere, and it wouldn't have helped the many poor people in state programs that still have asset tests. The Affordable Care Act eliminates the Medicaid asset test for those newly eligible for Medicaid, but this doesn't help Dave and Marcella, who are still under the state asset test because of her being in a previously eligible group, the disabled. If only California would follow the lead of half the states and lift its Medi-Cal asset test, it would make a huge difference in their lives.

Asset limits make low-income people's lives all the more precarious. At all income levels, a negative event such as job loss, health-related work limitations, or parental departure results in material hardship. But such hardship is much greater in asset-poor families, and the lower the family's income, the greater the impact of low assets.[16]

And asset limits affect the life chances of the next generation as well. Children are better off in families with savings: the offspring of low-income parents with high savings enjoy more economic mobility later in life than do those whose low-income parents had low savings.[17] But such savings are disallowed in most means-tested programs.

Poor Logan. It's bad enough that he was born prematurely and that his mom is permanently disabled. On top of all that, social policy rules dictate that he'll have to grow up in a low-income, low-savings household, shaping his life chances, perhaps holding him back for the rest of his life. We can only hope that policy makers will soon find a way to craft a safety net that doesn't trap children like him.

BENEFIT PHASEOUTS, CLIFFS, AND HUGE MARGINAL TAX RATES

Beyond the income and asset limits, there's not much incentive to earn more money, because social assistance recipients will lose most of that earning power as their benefits fall away. As they leave social assistance for paid work and their income rises, even modestly, they lose their eligibility for program after program.

Benefits in some programs phase out slowly. For example, SSI recipients who begin working lose $1 in benefits for every $2 they earn, until the benefit disappears. Twenty-seven-year-old Brad Crelia has an incurable hereditary blood disorder that inhibits his ability to work a regular full-time job. Like Marcella, he receives SSI. He would like to work when he's physically able, but is only allowed to earn $85 per month without penalty. Beyond that, he faces an effective 50 percent marginal tax rate as his SSI diminishes, and he loses SSI altogether when his income reaches $1,097 per month, just above the poverty line.[18]

Other programs, such as Medicaid and CHIP, have an eligibility cliff: earn one more dollar in income, and you lose eligibility for public health insurance altogether. This is the essence of the "means test" imposed by all social assistance programs: as your means rise, you fail the test. These benefit phaseouts and falloffs are essentially huge marginal taxes on those exiting social assistance for work. They provide a powerful disincentive, because the effective cost of working is so very high.

Yet these phaseouts, cliffs, and huge marginal tax rates aren't failures of means-tested programs alone. Recipients are trapped in poverty also because of failings at the boundaries between social assistance, other social supports, and jobs. If jobs or other social programs reliably provided health insurance or child care, transitions out of social assistance wouldn't impose such steep costs to the affected individuals. The problem is that on one side, we try diligently to minimize assistance programs by keeping their scope limited and clearly bounded. But this tight bounding means that people often exit means-tested programs—and do so abruptly—when they are still poor. On the other side, we have social programs and jobs that fail to provide the working poor with adequate wages or needed protections. If only one or the other existed, people would exit social assistance without the steep costs described here. But because both poor wages and meager protections exist together, leaving social assistance often means falling into a chasm.

Consider what happens when a single-parent household with two children increases its income from $10,000 to $40,000—from half the poverty line to double. This household consequently loses 29 percent of the $30,000 in additional earnings to federal and state taxes (Social Security payroll taxes and reduced Earned Income Tax Credit). If the family had been enrolled in the more widely available means-tested programs such as SNAP, Medicaid, and CHIP, which typically have no waiting lists, it would lose 55 percent of the additional earnings to taxes and reduced benefits. And if it had additionally been enrolled in the waiting-list programs of TANF and housing assistance, it would lose 80 percent.[19] That is, every additional dollar earned yields only 45 cents, or even as little as 20 cents as taxes increase and benefits fall away—the highest marginal tax rates faced by anyone in our society, far higher than what CEOs or investment tycoons at the top pay.

Faced with these huge effective marginal tax rates, why make the transition from social assistance to work if it means losing the family's Medicaid benefits? Why seek a higher-paying job if it means a lower food stamp benefit and Earned Income Tax Credit refund?

For that matter, why get married? EITC, CHIP, and sometimes Medicaid benefits extend relatively far up the income ladder. However, when two modest-income people marry, their combined incomes can push them out of eligibility, and their increased taxes and lost benefits combine for the high effective marginal tax rates described above. The Medicaid and CHIP health insurance benefits are particularly valuable, since many low- and moderate-income people have no other means of getting health coverage. So why marry? As economist

Eugene Steuerle puts it, "Not getting married is the major tax shelter for low- and moderate-income households with children."[20]

As a result of weak social provisions apart from social assistance and few employer-provided benefits in low-wage jobs, work imposes huge costs. Sociologists Kathryn Edin and Laura Lein interviewed hundreds of single mothers in two categories—those who left welfare for low-wage jobs and those who remained on public aid. They found that low-income working women, facing the loss of benefits, were in many ways worse off than those who stayed on welfare. Although the mothers with jobs had higher self-esteem than those on welfare, the toll on their families was profound. The working families were somewhat less likely to lack food or to go hungry, but they experienced greater core hardships overall (housing problems, utility cutoffs, inadequate winter clothes) and were much more likely to lack medical coverage. Compared with the welfare mothers, the working women were squeezed by greater expenses for child care, transportation, and clothing on the one hand and lost eligibility for social supports on the other. At the same time, the working mothers had less time to meet those gaps with supplemental work than did the welfare mothers, who typically made ends meet with either under-the-counter work such as child care or covert contributions from relatives and boyfriends. The working mothers also had less contact with their children than did the welfare mothers, and worried about the quality of the care their children received (often from informal caregivers).[21]

Edin and Lein performed their fieldwork before the 1996 welfare reform. What has changed since then is that many single mothers no longer have the choice of staying at home: they have to get jobs in order to get welfare. And such low-wage workers face the same difficulties Edin and Lein catalogued: dead-end jobs but greater expenses, paired with lost eligibility for other supports. The enactment of CHIP in 1997 means that the children of the working poor can get health insurance, but it doesn't take much income for the parents themselves to become ineligible for Medicaid in most states.[22] And the availability of affordable child care for mothers now forced to work remains a concern.

Consider the huge marginal tax rate confronted by those enrolled in Share of Cost Medi-Cal, as we originally thought Dave and Marcella were (and would be again, if Dave made much more money). Above the modest amount such individuals are allowed to live on, they must pay all their remaining income in share of cost. And if they make more money, their share of cost simply increases, dollar for dollar: a 100 percent tax. The rational person would dial down his or her work hours to avoid the share of cost altogether, as Dave did while we (erroneously) thought he and Marcella were in that program.

In the perverse world of means-tested programs, work doesn't pay.

ADMINISTRATIVE BARRIERS AND RED TAPE

As the first two (and last two) chapters of this book reveal, Marcella has faced a real runaround trying to secure the benefits she needs—difficult application procedures, red tape, denial of benefits. She and Dave have had to fight every step of the way. And she's a *deserving* beneficiary. If she were a TANF mom, she could face fingerprinting, intrusive questions about her sexual history, and drug testing before getting benefits.[23]

STIGMA

And if all else fails, there's stigma. The idea is to make applying for and enrolling in means-tested programs so unpalatable that people will stomach any alternative, including a low-wage job, even if it is economically inferior. That so many of the eligible don't even try to sign up shows how effective stigma is.

THE POVERTY TRAP AND ITS PERVERSITIES

Means-tested programs force hard choices on their recipients. Millions of Americans in need face the same dilemma as Dave and Marcella: the requirement to stay poor to get the supports on which they depend. The disabled in particular can face an "extreme choice" between assistance and work, as Massachusetts-based Medicaid expert Tony Dreyfus says.[24] Even if they are capable of work, many of the disabled dare not, both because they would lose their crucial Medicaid coverage and because their SSI cash benefits would be reduced as they earned income. Their stark choice: they must remain poor or else "give up all government support," a "poverty trap" that discourages work and that leaves many of the disabled below the poverty line.[25]

A similar poverty trap ensnares other poor people as well. What's perverse is that policy makers rail against a "cycle of poverty," but then design programs that *create* a cycle of poverty. An old debate from the 1960s concerned whether a "culture of poverty" existed among the poor, a distinctive set of attitudes and behaviors such as helplessness and dependence that kept them mired in poverty and in need of social assistance.[26] The contemporary version of this concept focuses on the perceived shortcomings of the poor as individuals. For example, in discussing low rates of economic mobility in the United States compared with Europe, conservative writer Stuart Butler attributes the "stickiness" of Americans' incomes—those born at the top or the bottom of the income spectrum are more likely to remain in that position in the United States than in other rich nations—to parental characteristics. "Parents who lack the personal qualities required for success—thrift, honesty, perseverance, a strong work ethic, and so on—often have children who lack them, too," he writes, and "it is this 'stickiness' of habits that contributes to the *causes* of poverty and low income mobility."[27]

This debate about whether poverty has individual or systemic causes is an old one, and is emblematic of the basic disagreements between conservatives and liberals. But an examination of policy design suggests high systemic barriers no matter what an individual's personal traits are. It's really hard to leave poverty for work when benefit phaseouts mean that work doesn't pay, and when eligibility cutoffs—particularly harsh in health care—mean total loss of supports. And what's offered by jobs and other social programs doesn't make up the difference.

The twisted logic continues in the impact of program designs on families. In the effort to isolate benefits to a narrow definition of the truly needy, means-tested programs undermine the value of work, the possibility of monetary help from extended family, and the incentives for family formation in ways that would appear to violate conservatives' concerns about the work ethic and family values. These programs as currently structured induce people to work less. They lead people to get divorced or never to marry in the first place. They prohibit recipients' extended families from helping financially. And they create a lot of intergenerational collateral damage: in the case of Marcella, Dave, and Logan, Medi-Cal's design has created not just one asset-poor person but three. Is that really the policy makers' intent?

WHAT CAN BE DONE

If means-tested programs are so riddled with problems, should we just get rid of them? Some conservatives might hope so—and they've gotten their wish with regard to TANF. It is now such a small program, serving so few people, that it's a minor part of social assistance.[28]

But in truth, the need for social protections is not going away. The real solution is to improve the designs of means-tested programs and to address the problems at the boundaries between social assistance, jobs, and other social supports.

Steurele suggests revamping the design of social assistance by taking an "integrated approach" to social policy and tax reform that would recognize their interrelatedness, rather than setting policies one at a time. He also recommends making implicit tax rates more explicit and setting a maximum marginal tax rate so that the falloff in benefits as a person leaves assistance for work is less steep.[29] Lifting or eliminating asset limits would bolster the financial security of low-income people as well.[30]

Yet another idea is to improve conditions in low-wage jobs. Many states and localities have minimum wages higher than the federal minimum. The Affordable Care Act includes tax breaks for small employers who offer health insurance. However, it simply may not be economically feasible for low-wage employers to offer more benefits. Strong public programs are needed.

Thus, a third idea is to bolster other social supports. Scholars such as Theda Skocpol advocate extending to new areas the universalistic model of social policy that has been so successful in public education, Social Security, and the G.I. Bill.[31] Universal policies recognize that nearly everyone, not just the poor, needs help with the big-ticket items in life. They give support to all with these needs, providing considerable financial relief to the middle class while helping lower-income people in a stigma-free way. In addition, they make it easier to leave poverty, because they don't have the benefit cliffs and phaseouts that means-tested programs do. Additional areas in which such a program design might be used include universal child care and preschool, universal paid family leave, and universal health insurance. To this list I would add a social insurance program for long-term care so that the disabled of any age don't have to impoverish themselves to get assistance.

California's experience with paid family leave illustrates the advantages of the universal approach. The program is funded by a payroll tax on all jobholders—but has most benefited low-wage workers, whose employers typically hadn't offered paid leave previously.[32] Adding universal programs in areas like health insurance and child care would not only ease the transition from social assistance to work but also address economic insecurity across the income spectrum and engender wide political support.[33]

PUTTING THE MEAN IN MEANS-TESTED POLICY

The structure of American means-tested programs helps keep people poor. As we've seen, not only do they have to be poor to get help for life's risks, but they have to stay poor. Low benefit levels keep program recipients far below the poverty line and make sheer survival a struggle. Asset tests add to families' financial precariousness, prohibiting them from saving for emergencies and other needs. And there is little incentive to leave social assistance for work. Those who wish to escape poverty face a daunting task to begin with, and benefit phaseouts and eligibility cutoffs create huge additional barriers as income rises, such as steep marginal tax rates. In essence, work doesn't pay when you lose 50, 60, 80 cents of every dollar you earn. Or 100 percent, in the case of Share of Cost Medi-Cal. All in the name of tightly targeting these programs and making sure they're worse than the worst job out there.

The result is a system rife with perversities and self-contradictions, from discouraging saving, marriage, and work to encouraging divorce and bad child care arrangements. Program designs are meant to make assistance less desirable than work, but then the inadequacies of low-wage jobs and other social welfare programs make work an untenable option as well. Poor Americans are trapped. In the context of larger systemic failings, the programs meant to give them a helping hand instead keep a boot on their throats.

5 | THE FIFTY DIFFERENT WORLDS OF SOCIAL ASSISTANCE

The good news is that Marcella and Dave live in California. The bad news is that Marcella and Dave live in California. The state is more generous than others in some ways: it has the Access for Infants and Mothers health insurance program for middle-income pregnant women, which allowed Marcella and Dave to contemplate having a baby in the first place. The income cutoff for CHIP, the public health insurance program for children whose family is uninsured, is a relatively generous 250 percent of the federal poverty level ($47,725 in 2012). With an income of $39,000, Marcella and Dave could have a baby, secure in the knowledge that it would have health insurance. Medi-Cal allows them to retain more assets than some states' Medicaid programs, whose asset tests are even more stringent. California also is one of only three states with paid family and medical leave, which allowed Dave to take time off from work after the accident.

In other regards, California is less generous. In many other states, Marcella and Dave would be allowed to save for Logan's college education through a 529 college fund without threatening Marcella's Medicaid eligibility.[1] In a number of other states, they'd be allowed to save for retirement, and Marcella wouldn't have had to liquidate her 401(k) savings to qualify for public health insurance. Indeed, twenty-four states use no asset test for Medicaid. In these states, Marcella and Dave could do it all: save for retirement, college, and emergencies, and Dave could drive a safe car to work. But not in California, where they happen to live.

The experience of the poor in means-tested programs varies tremendously across states. Unlike the major social insurance programs,

Social Security and Medicare, which are run by the federal government with the same eligibility guidelines and benefit levels nationwide, many social assistance programs are run jointly by the federal government and the states; the states determine who is eligible and what kinds of benefits they get. Interstate variation springs up even for programs featuring a greater federal role and uniform benefits nationwide, such as food stamps: because state outreach efforts differ so much, enrollment rates vary, even if benefit levels and eligibility do not. Decentralization is one of the most consequential characteristics of American social policy,[2] and one that stands out in cross-national comparison. In other rich nations, eligibility and benefits do not vary merely as a function of location, as they do in the United States.

State control over means-tested programs and the resultant variation in outcomes originate in the racial and gender politics of the past. Plenty of contemporary arguments for state control and variation exist as well, which this chapter will consider. But in the end, the fact that the same family can have a vastly different experience based solely on where it lives raises questions about the effectiveness, desirability, and even morality of this variation. State control produces many of the poverty traps we saw in the previous chapter as well. In sum, a person's public policy experience is a sheer accident of geography. Is that just?

THE ORIGINS OF STATE CONTROL
IN MEANS-TESTED PROGRAMS

States have always played an important role in social assistance.[3] Before the Great Depression and World War II, which greatly expanded the size and role of the federal government, state and local governments collected far more tax revenue and were responsible for more functions than the government in Washington, DC. Indeed, a number of states had workers' compensation programs, old-age pensions, and mothers' pensions (which supported poor single mothers with children at home) long before the New Deal instituted programs for the aged, blind, poor, and unemployed. Because these earlier programs were entirely state run, states had a great deal of discretion over eligibility and benefits, and were loath to give up these powers to the federal government. In particular, southern states used the differential application of assistance programs to reinforce an economic system based on black agricultural labor. For example, mothers' pensions weren't available in counties with the highest concentrations of African Americans in order to maximize the number of available workers.[4]

The vast economic dislocation of the Great Depression laid bare the inadequacy of state social assistance programs and the need for a new system of social protections. However, moves by the Roosevelt administration to craft a set of programs to provide these protections, which became the Social Security Act of 1935, threatened the political economy of the South. As hard-hit as the South was by the Depression—many of its states had to scale back their social assistance programs greatly—federal provision of Unemployment Insurance or mothers' pensions posed a profound threat. These funds would provide a stream of monetary aid to black agricultural workers and domestics outside the control of the white planter elite, thereby threatening the underlying racial and class structure of the southern economy and society.[5]

Southern congressmen used their dominance of key congressional committees to maintain the racial order and to reinforce state sovereignty and control. The social insurance programs of the Social Security Act of 1935—Old Age Insurance (what we think of today as "Social Security") and Unemployment Insurance—initially covered only workers in "commerce and industry," thus excluding occupations where African Americans were concentrated, such as farm laborers and domestics.[6] These racially discriminatory effects gradually diminished as more occupations were brought into the system. By the 1970s, Social Security in particular became a virtually "universal" program for which most retired workers were eligible, one that helped alleviate poverty in old age among the majority of income and ethnic/racial groups.

The legacy of racial politics and states' rights proved far more enduring when it came to social assistance. Beyond the new social insurance policies, the Social Security Act also contained two social assistance programs: Old Age Assistance (cash payments for the impoverished elderly) and Aid to Dependent Children (ADC, later AFDC and then replaced by TANF—that is, cash "welfare" payments to poor families with children, the successor to mothers' pensions). Unlike Old Age Insurance, Old Age Assistance and ADC were not purely federal programs, at the insistence of southern congressmen. Instead, the federal government would pay a portion of program costs, but states would retain operational control and set eligibility criteria and benefit levels. These representatives further insisted that a provision that ADC payments provide "a reasonable subsistence compatible with decency and health" be stripped from the legislation.[7] Although Old Age Assistance was eventually federalized as Supplemental Security Income (SSI) in 1972, the hybrid federal-state design of ADC persisted. The phenomena that we observe today—state discretion over social assistance, widely varying program parameters, and the failure of many social assistance programs to meet underlying needs—hark back to this founding era and the legacy of racial politics.

When the nation's public health insurance programs were created in 1965, the same dichotomies between insurance and assistance and between federal and joint federal-state responsibility were adopted. Medicare, for senior citizens, would be a federal-level social insurance program with nationally uniform eligibility criteria and benefits. In contrast, Medicaid, for the poor, would adopt AFDC's hybrid federal-state structure: the federal government would pay part of the cost and stipulate minimum eligibility criteria and benefits, but states could determine the scope of benefits and eligible populations beyond those minima as well as set provider reimbursement levels (which ultimately affected recipients' access to health care).[8] Program funding differed as well. Medicare financing came entirely from federal and recipient sources: a payroll tax for Part A hospital insurance, and general federal tax revenues and monthly premiums for Part B supplemental medical insurance. In contrast, states were on the hook for part of Medicaid's financing, which they shared with the federal government. That is, states had to spend their own dollars in order to receive federal matching money. Despite a matching formula that provided a greater federal contribution in poorer states, the robustness of the program would nonetheless come to depend on each state's fiscal capacity.

To this day, means-tested social assistance programs bear the marks of their birth in the crucible of American racial politics and states' rights.[9] For our purposes, what matters is that the states, both then and now, play a central role in these programs. Today, state fiscal capacity and to a lesser extent ideology are what shape social assistance provision. But the result is the same: vast interstate differences in policies and outcomes.

CROSS-STATE VARIATION IN MEANS-TESTED PROGRAMS

Variation is evident along nearly every parameter of each program. States vary in whether they even have a given program. Although every state participates in TANF, Medicaid, and CHIP, less than half the states offer a state-level Earned Income Tax Credit to supplement the federal program. Southern states adopted Medicaid slowly, and Arizona waited until 1982. Eligibility varies dramatically as well, meaning that an individual at a given income or asset level qualifies for a program in one state but not another. And what counts as income and assets differs too. Moreover, the size and scope of benefits vary dramatically, from the size of monthly checks in the cash programs to the scope of covered medical benefits in Medicaid. Take-up rates—the proportions of eligible people actually enrolled in each program—also vary across states. The result of all these differences is considerable variation in adequacy: in the proportion of poor people who actually receive benefits and in the ability of those benefits to meet basic human needs. A brief review of selected programs illustrates just how much policies differ from one state to the next.

Temporary Assistance for Needy Families

Forty years ago, four in five poor children received welfare; now four in five poor children do not.[10] Behind this long-term decline in the size and reach of the program, however, is considerable variation across the states. As the bars in figure 5.1 show, the proportion of poor children receiving welfare in 2009 was above 40 percent in Washington, Hawaii, and Massachusetts, above 50 percent in California and Maine, but below 10 percent in Florida, Colorado, Illinois, North Carolina, Oklahoma, Mississippi, Arkansas, Louisiana, Georgia, Texas, Wyoming, and Idaho. That is, in a dozen states, less than one in ten poor children received cash assistance. And nearly all states covered fewer poor children than they had in 1969, denoted by the solid line.

There is also considerable variation in the size of TANF benefits (fig. 5.2). Among the lower forty-eight states, the maximum monthly TANF cash benefit in July 2011 for a family of three varied from $788 in New York, $714 in California, and $640 in Vermont to just $185 in Tennessee and $170 in Mississippi.[11] In twenty-two states, the maximum benefit provided an income less than one-fourth of the poverty line; in a few states at the bottom, the most a recipient could get from TANF was barely over 10 percent of the poverty line. Per person,

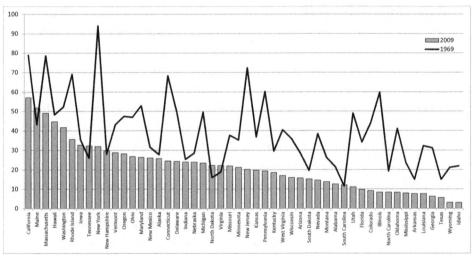

Figure 5.1 Proportion of Poor Children Who Receive Welfare (AFDC/TANF) by State, 1969 and 2009

Source: House Ways and Means Committee, *2011 Greenbook*, table 7-13

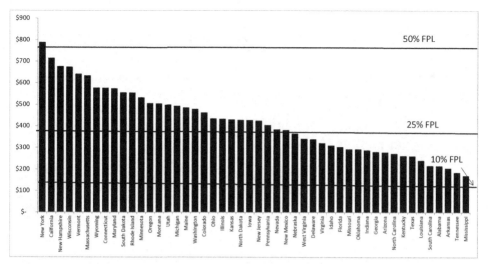

Figure 5.2 Maximum Monthly TANF Benefit for a Family of Three by State, July 2011
Source: Urban Institute, "Welfare Rules Databook," August 2012, 90–91.

that's $2 per day—the World Bank's definition of poverty in developing countries.[12]

This variation in TANF benefits, and their low level, persists even after controlling for differences in the cost of living. Figure 5.3 divides the maximum TANF benefit for a family of three by the budget a three-person family needs to sustain a modest lifestyle in each state.[13] In most states, TANF provides less than 10 percent of what a family needs to live. And even after accounting for cost-of-living differences, the low-benefit states in figure 5.2 remain on the bottom.

As in other means-tested programs, asset tests vary tremendously. Five states have no asset test or limit in order to qualify for TANF. In those states with asset limits, the thresholds range from $1,000 (as in Georgia, Texas, and Washington, among others) to $10,000 (Delaware), and are typically $2,000 or $3,000. Some states exempt only one vehicle from this asset test, while others exempt all vehicles owned by the household.[14]

Other regulations vary as well. Some states try to divert families from becoming recipients in the first place by giving them a lump-

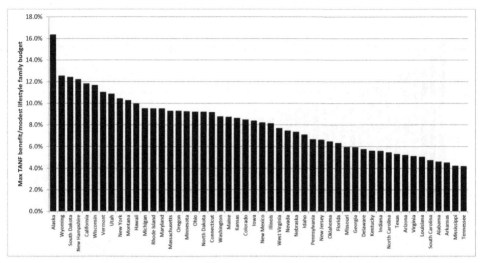

Figure 5.3 TANF Benefits Adjusted for Cost-of-Living Differences across States

Note: Figure shows the maximum TANF benefit for a family of three divided by the budget needed to sustain a modest lifestyle in the largest city in each state for a one-adult, two-child family.

Sources: TANF figures from Urban Institute, "Welfare Rules Databook," August 2012, 90–91. Family budget from Economic Policy Institute's Family Budget Calculator, http://www.epi .org/resources/budget/.

sum cash payment for their immediate needs rather than signing them up for a TANF benefit; those who choose that payment are barred from applying for TANF for some months. The size of the lump-sum payments and the length of the ineligibility period vary across states.[15] Some states require applicants to be engaged in a job search at the point of their TANF application, while some do not.[16] Some states include all or a portion of the income of grandparents and/or stepparents living in the household in the income test for eligibility, while some do not.[17] States also differ in their TANF work requirements, with different rules for which TANF adults are work-eligible, what constitutes "work," and what the sanctions are for refusing to comply.[18] Sanctions for violating the work requirement or other program rules range from temporary benefit reduction to complete ineligibility.[19]

To sum up, TANF rules and benefits differ widely across states, even across near neighbors. A stepparent's income is included in the income test in Iowa but not in Kansas; a grandparent's income is included in New Hampshire but not in Vermont. A family with $2,000 in assets would be eligible for TANF in Oregon but not in Washington. Idaho requires applicants to be engaged in a job search to receive benefits, while Montana does not. In Mississippi, the highest sanction for failing to comply with the work requirement is total loss of benefits and permanent ineligibility for TANF, while in Arkansas the case is merely closed until the family is in compliance for two weeks. A family's experience depends entirely on the state in which it happens to live.

Medicaid

Perhaps the vast differences in TANF from state to state should come as no surprise; cash assistance for the poor has always been the least popular component of the American welfare state.[20] But what about health insurance for the poor? Surveys show that Americans think of health care differently—as not quite a right, as people in other countries believe, but at least as something that shouldn't be withheld, particularly compared with other types of benefits such as cash assistance.[21] Knowing this, do Medicaid requirements and benefits vary less across states than TANF parameters do?

The answer is no, for the most part.

Federal law requires states to cover certain groups, including pregnant women and children under the age of six who are below 133 percent of the poverty line; children aged six to eighteen below 100 percent of the poverty line; and a few others.[22] Beyond these required categories, states can choose to expand eligibility to higher-income groups. For example, all but 4 states cover children in Medicaid or CHIP up to 200 percent of the federal poverty level. However, there is much greater variation in the coverage of adults. In 2012, 41 states covered pregnant women above the required 133 percent of the poverty line, ranging up to 250 percent of the poverty line in Connecticut and Maryland, 275 percent in Minnesota, and 300 percent in Iowa and Wisconsin.[23] In 2013, 18 states covered the working parents of Medicaid-eligible children above the poverty line, while 16 states limited eligibility to parents below half the poverty line.[24] The Affordable Care Act would have required states to cover all persons under 138 percent of the federal poverty level, but a Supreme Court ruling made this coverage expansion optional; as of 2014, childless adults can join Medicaid in some states but not in others.

The Medicaid asset test varies considerably. Twenty-four states have no asset test for Medicaid; Dave and Marcella could have savings had they lived in one of them. Among the 26 states with asset tests, most limit assets to $2,000 or $3,000, although limits range from $1,000 to $30,000 (see fig. 5.4). Some states count 529 college savings plans or personal retirement savings toward the asset test, while some do

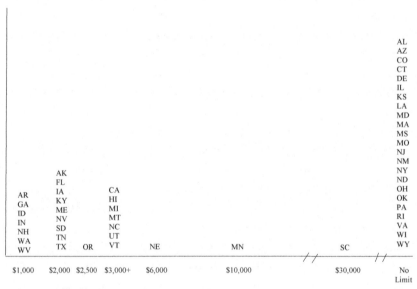

Figure 5.4 Medicaid Asset Limit by State, 2012

Source: Aleta Sprague, "Lifting the Medicaid Asset Test: A Step in the Right Direction," New America Foundation, April 9, 2012, http://assets.newamerica.net/blogposts/2012/ lifting_the_medicaid_asset_test_a_step_in_the_right_direction-66214.

not.[25] Some exempt one vehicle from the asset test, while others exempt all the household's vehicles. In those states, Dave wouldn't have had to sell his hobby cars.

Federal law stipulates that all state Medicaid programs must cover certain services: inpatient and outpatient hospital services, physician services, laboratory and X-ray services, home health services, nursing facility services, and several others.[26] Other benefits are optional for states, and their provision varies considerably. States don't have to cover prescription drugs, though all do, to widely varying extents. Some states cover a thirty-four-day supply with a stipulated number of refills, while others limit the number of covered prescriptions per month (from two in Washington to eight in Louisiana).[27] The federal government requires states to provide dental services, eye exams, and eyeglasses to children in Medicaid, but adult coverage is optional.[28] Other optional benefits include physical therapy, occupational therapy, respiratory care services, prosthetics, hospice care, and so on.[29] Some states offer them, and some don't.

One reason for such wide variation in eligibility and benefits is that Medicaid is a very expensive program to run, and poorer states can afford less. States split the cost with the federal government; the feds provide more funding to the poorer states, as measured by per capita income. A poor state receives $2.85 in federal funds for every dollar it spends of its own funds, while richer states only receive $1.00.[30] But getting the federal match still means spending a state dollar, which poor states are less likely to have.[31] The inverse matching formula is meant to incentivize states to enroll more of their low-income groups in Medicaid. But in reality, poorer states often can't afford to be more generous, even with the greater federal match.

The result is that even for health insurance, the experience of the poor varies dramatically across states and across time with states' fluctuating fiscal circumstances.[32] A low-income person from one of the federally required groups can get Medicaid in California with $2,500 in assets, but not in Nevada. With $5,000 in assets, such an individual is eligible in Minnesota but not in Michigan. A pregnant woman with income at 150 percent of the federal poverty level is eligible for Medicaid in Georgia but not in Alabama; at 200 percent of poverty, she would be eligible in New Mexico but not in Arizona. The working parent of a Medicaid-eligible child in Arkansas can get Medicaid for herself only if her income is less than 16 percent of the federal poverty level (that's Nigeria-level income), while in Wisconsin she can get Medicaid if her income is up to 200 percent of the poverty line (that's one-third of American households). An adult Medicaid recipient can get eyeglasses in Texas but not in Oklahoma; Tennessee provides one pair of glasses after cataract surgery, while in Utah the only Medicaid adults who can get eyeglasses are pregnant women. In a Massachusetts Medicaid family, a child can get a filling in any tooth, but his mom can get a filling only in her twelve front teeth, not in her molars. Between 2010 and 2012, she would have been out of luck entirely, because state budget cuts eliminated most adult dental benefits altogether.[33] And on and absurdly on. As with TANF, how you fare is an accident of time and place.

Children's Health Insurance Program

Perhaps these disparities across states aren't surprising in TANF and Medicaid—after all, both programs, or their precursors, were born in eras whose public policies bore the marks of racial politics. What about a "modern" program like the Children's Health Insurance Program, signed into law in 1997? Surely that program doesn't suffer the same degree of interstate variation. And yet it does.

CHIP provides health insurance for children whose families lack coverage but whose incomes are too high for Medicaid. It is funded jointly by the federal and state governments (using the same matching rate as Medicaid, plus a 15 percent sweetener to encourage state participation), but states determine eligibility and other program parameters. By 2012, nearly all states—forty-seven—had eliminated their asset test for CHIP,[34] but they still set income thresholds, with the income cutoff for eligibility varying from just 160 percent of the federal poverty level in North Dakota to 400 percent in New York. As with TANF, the variation in income cutoffs is far greater than actual cost-of-living differences across states.[35] A child whose parents make $40,000 is eligible for CHIP in Tennessee but not in Kentucky. In a $50,000 household, a child is eligible in Connecticut but not in Rhode Island; at $35,000, a child is eligible in South Dakota but not in North Dakota. In Arizona, an uninsured child above the poverty level is out of luck altogether: the state closed its CHIP program to new enrollment in December 2009.[36] What happens to the Logans of Arizona?

In addition, many program rules beyond basic eligibility vary: whether the program is separate from Medicaid or combined with it; whether the benefits are the same as for Medicaid; whether a family must pay a monthly premium or a copayment. Thirty-eight states have a waiting period, a length of time a child is required to be uninsured before allowed to enroll in CHIP, which varies from one to twelve months.[37] States impose waiting periods because they fear that parents will drop employer-provided insurance to enroll their children in CHIP. There is little evidence that parents engage in such behavior, however.[38] And waiting periods are antithetical to the purpose of insuring children. Imagine if Logan were born in a state with a twelve-month waiting period. Is he supposed to go without medical care or checkups for the first year of his life, the most important and delicate developmental stage? As with the older means-tested programs, CHIP eligibility and other rules differ depending on where the child happens to live.

State-Level Earned Income Tax Credits

Another type of means-tested program with pronounced variation is the state-level Earned Income Tax Credit. The federal EITC began in 1975, intended to offset the income and payroll taxes paid by working families and to increase their take-home pay. In 1987, Maryland became the first state to offer its own EITC, and as of 2011, twenty-three states and the District of Columbia have created their own.[39] The state EITCs supplement their federal counterpart, similarly enhancing take-home pay and reducing poverty by refunding part of the state and local taxes paid by lower-income workers. This is an important innovation, because state taxes have been consuming a greater proportion of low- and middle-income taxpayers' earnings over time.[40] With the advent of EITCs, the number of states imposing income taxes on workers below the poverty line fell by half.[41] A few local governments—Montgomery County in Maryland, San Francisco, and New York City—have enacted EITCs as well.

As with other income-targeted programs, interstate variation in the EITC programs is substantial. Most states use federal eligibility rules and set their EITC as a proportion of the federal credit. However, that proportion varies hugely, from 3.5 to 40 percent.[42] For 2012, Marcella and Dave received a $3,200 federal EITC credit. If they lived in Washington, DC, they would have received an additional $1,280 back; in Minnesota it would have been $1,056. They would have received $192 in nearby Oregon or $320 in Washington. But they received nothing, because California doesn't have an EITC. Thus, not only does access to means-tested programs vary, but so does the take-home pay of lower-wage workers, all because of differences in state policies.

Supplemental Security Income

SSI is a federal program providing cash assistance to poor elderly, blind, and disabled people, but most states supplement the federal benefit with their own additional payments (the exceptions are Arizona, North Dakota, Mississippi, and West Virginia). As a result, actual SSI benefit levels vary across states. It's difficult to illustrate the range of supplemental payments, because states don't use uniform categories or make payments to the same types of individuals (some states assist SSI recipients living independently, while others provide aid only to those in institutions). A few snapshots: an SSI recipient living independently in the community would receive a $10 monthly supplement in Maine and $14 in Michigan, but $168 in Connecticut.[43]

And then there's California—again, a state unusually generous in some regards, unusually penurious in others. Although SSI recipients by definition are poor, they aren't eligible for food stamps in California, the only state in the nation with that stipulation.[44] Instead, the state adds extra money for food to the SSI monthly payment. But the state supplement fails to make up the difference. In 2012, the combined federal and state SSI benefit for a disabled individual living independently in California was $854.[45] In Massachusetts, the combined benefit was only $812, but recipients there are allowed to apply for SNAP as well for a total of $944.[46] Thus, California's "generosity" leaves disabled persons with lower total benefits—$1,080 less over the course of a year. That said, given that Dave blanched when I had mentioned food stamps, perhaps California's method of boosting SSI instead is more palatable and helpful to him and Marcella, even if it means fewer dollars than from states allowing SNAP for the disabled. If only these programs for the poor weren't so stigmatized.

Food Stamps

Finally, even in a federal program with uniform benefits nationwide, there's variation across states along other dimensions. For example, the take-up rate in the food stamp program (SNAP) varies substantially, likely owing to different administrative procedures and outreach efforts among the states. SNAP may be federal, but it's local and state social workers who inform people about their eligibility and sign them up—or not. In 2006, 67 percent of those eligible for food stamps participated in the program, but the participation rate varied from 98 percent in Missouri to just 50 percent in California (fig. 5.5).[47]

HOW DAVE AND MARCELLA WOULD
HAVE FARED IN DIFFERENT STATES

As the above examples illustrate, the recipients of means-tested programs can be treated quite differently, depending on the state in which they happen to live. Just a few miles and a few dollars of income or assets can mean the difference between being insured and being uninsured. Living in one state rather than the another can result in differences of hundreds, even thousands of dollars in cash assistance or state tax credits.

Marcella and Dave would have a very different experience if they

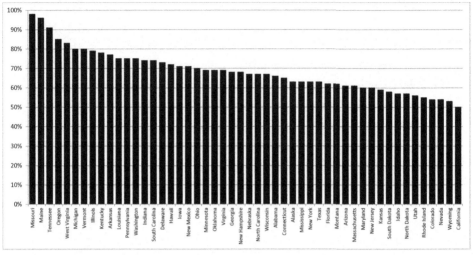

Figure 5.5 Food Stamp Take-Up Rate by State, 2006

Note: Figure shows percentage of eligible individuals enrolled in SNAP by state.
Source: Cunnyngham et al., "State Food Stamp Participation Rates in 2006," Mathematica
Policy Research for USDA Food and Nutrition Service, November 2008.

lived in a state other than California. Table 5.1 summarizes the provisions of several programs across eight states from around the country. Since Dave's pre-accident income was just under 200 percent of the federal poverty line, Logan would be eligible for CHIP in six of the states, but he would have been uninsured in North Dakota and Idaho, which have lower income cutoffs. In California, Dave and Marcella can have only $3,150 in assets to be eligible for Medicaid, but they would have been worse off in Texas, Tennessee, and Idaho, which have even lower asset caps. Conversely, if they lived in New York, Wisconsin, or North Dakota, which have no such caps, they wouldn't have had to liquidate their assets in order for Marcella to have health insurance, and they could live with the security of an emergency fund and retirement savings. California supplies a $190 state supplement to SSI recipients like Marcella, but no food stamp eligibility. In contrast, other states allow SSI recipients to apply for food stamps, but the state SSI supplements vary substantially—from $130 in Wisconsin to $52 in Idaho and $23 in New York. In Nebraska, the supplement

Table 5.1 How Marcella, Dave, and baby Logan would have fared in other states

	CA	NY	WI	NE	TX	TN	ND	ID
Baby CHIP eligible	Yes	Yes	Yes	Yes	Yes	Yes	No	No
Medicaid asset test	$3,150	No test	No test	$6,025	$2,000	$2,000	No test	$1,000
State SSI supplement	$190*	$23	$130	$5	None	None	None	$52
State EITC	None	30%	4%	10%	None	None	None	None
Paid family leave	Yes	No	No	No	No	No	No	No
Personal care services	280 hrs/mo=	"Service provided at 2 levels"	50 visits/yr=	40 hrs/wk=	50 hrs/wk=	None before 2010	300 hrs/mo=	10 hrs/wk=
	9.3 hrs/day		.14 visits/day	5.7 hrs/day	1.7 hrs/day		10.0 hrs/day	1.4 hrs/day

*But no food stamp eligibility for SSI recipients in California.

Sources: CHIP: "Children's Health Insurance Program: Upper Income Limits as of September 22, 2011," www.medicaid.gov. Medicaid: Aleta Sprague, "Lifting the Medicaid Asset Test: A Step in the Right Direction," New America Foundation, April 9, 2012. SSI: Social Security Administration, "State Assistance Programs for SSI Recipients, January 2011." EITC: Nicholas Johnson and Erica Williams, "A Hand Up: How State Earned Income Tax Credits Help Working Families Escape Poverty in 2011," Center on Budget and Policy Priorities, April 2011. Medicaid personal care service hours: Kaiser Family Foundation, State Health Facts, Medicaid Benefits: Personal Care Services, as of October 2010.

Note: State EITC is expressed as percentage of the federal EITC credit. In Wisconsin, state EITC is 4 percent of the federal credit in one-child households. In Texas, SSI state supplements are available only to those living in a Medicaid facility.

is just $5 (why even bother?). The remaining states don't supplement federal SSI payments at all. Dave and Marcella could expect a state EITC credit worth 4 percent of their federal credit in Wisconsin, 10 percent in Nebraska, and a whopping 30 percent in New York, but in their home state of California they get nothing. But fortunately, in California Dave was allowed to take paid family leave from his job to spend time with Marcella and the baby after the accident— a policy that exists nowhere else except New Jersey and Rhode Island.[48]

In some ways, personal care assistance is the most valuable benefit Marcella receives, because it's so crucial for her daily life and because it's so expensive, with no source other than Medicaid. But here too state provisions vary vastly, with real implications for the disabled. California and North Dakota will provide up to nine or ten hours of personal care per day—a realistic amount for those who cannot eat, bathe, dress, use the toilet, or move from bed to wheelchair by themselves. In contrast, Wisconsin provides only fifty visits per year; until recently, Tennessee didn't provide home-based personal care services at all.[49] These states apparently assume that elderly and disabled individuals have relatives who can provide such care. But many do not, and how they are supposed to manage with one visit per week or no personal care assistance at all is hard to fathom. Dennis Heaphy, a prominent Massachusetts-based disability rights activist with three master's degrees, has turned down job offers in other states because they don't offer enough personal care attendant hours to meet his needs as a quadriplegic.[50] State variation has real consequences for people's lives.

WHAT HAPPENS IN THE STINGIEST STATES

Consider Tennessee. Because of a powerful nursing home lobby, virtually the only way for that state's disabled people to obtain personal care assistance if they had no relatives or their own resources was to live in a nursing home, not their own home.[51] It was "an inhumane system which made little fiscal sense to boot," Deborah Cunningham, executive director of the Memphis Center for Independent Living, told me.[52] In 2005, 97 percent of the elderly and disabled

Tennesseans getting long-term supports and services lived in nursing homes, while only 3 percent lived in the community.[53] Compared with all other states, "we were on the absolute bottom" in home- and community-based services, she added.

Disability rights activists tried for decades to loosen the nursing home industry's grip in Tennessee and to get the state to fund home-based services (Our Homes, Not Nursing Homes was one slogan). They conducted sit-ins and live-ins at the governor's office. Finally, in 2010 the state implemented an initiative to use some of its Medicaid money for in-home services. Disabled people began to leave nursing homes for their own communities, with Medicaid providing some transitional money for apartment deposits, furniture, and other housekeeping items as well. The proportion of elderly and disabled people receiving long-term supports and services in nursing homes decreased to 67 percent by 2013.[54]

But limitations remain. Cunningham related the story of one client who inherited a small sum when her father passed away. As a result, she lost her personal care services. The Memphis CIL appealed on her behalf, and she was able to get services restored after three months—but only for six days a week, not seven, as if "magically she doesn't need services on Sunday," as Cunningham put it. Progress in moving people into the community is slow, and the CIL is "kind of on guard" still, worried about policy backsliding in the future.

And then Cunningham told me a jaw-dropping story. Before the 2010 shift in policy, "people would come to the CIL looking for services, especially young people in nursing homes, saying, 'I want to get out of this hellhole.'" Given the lack of state funding for home-based personal care services, there wasn't much the Memphis CIL could do. But beginning in the early 1990s, it lit upon an idea. It set up an "underground railroad" with the disability rights group ADAPT in Denver, buying one-way plane tickets for Tennessee nursing home residents to escape to Colorado, where they could set up personal care assistance in a community apartment. "These people were so desperate to be free, to live like human beings, they left friends and family behind, and they've never been back," Cunningham said. The

CIL would raise the money by asking medical equipment suppliers to pitch in $100 here, $200 there. "In an afternoon, we could raise enough money for a ticket. We would provide a ride to the airport, and ADAPT and CIL leaders would meet them on the other end" and help them set up housekeeping. Over the next decade, at least sixteen people fled this way, including three of Cunningham's CIL staff members.[55]

One disabled nursing home resident who secured a Denver ticket through the Memphis CIL organized a group of friends to drive him to the airport. The director of his nursing home got wind of the plan and phoned Cunningham, saying, "If he tries to leave, I will have the state police bring him back, and I will accuse the friends of kidnapping." The CIL warned the friends in time, and they waited until the director left the premises to spirit away the disabled gentleman.

I almost can't believe what Deborah Cunningham told me. It's like the movie *Argo*, except the hostages are trying to escape American nursing homes, not the Islamic Revolution in Iran.

CONTEMPORARY ARGUMENTS FOR STATE CONTROL AND VARIATION

For good or ill, the experiences of social assistance beneficiaries depend greatly on where they live. The federated structure of the US government makes such variation possible. States have their own taxing and spending powers. Social program legislation has given them policy-setting responsibilities as well. The result is fifty different worlds of social assistance, with individuals of the same needs description being eligible for programs and getting certain benefits—or not—merely because of their location.

Advocates of policy decentralization argue that state control and interstate variation breed responsiveness, innovation, and efficiency.[56] The idea is that states compete with one another for both households and businesses that are mobile and that actively choose their location. In this view, firms locate where they believe the regulations, infrastructure, and other aspects of state business climate would be most conducive to their success. Individuals choose a state where the mix of services and taxes (and administration and regulation) best suits their preferences. Proponents of this view often use market analogies: in the same way that consumer choice induces competing businesses to offer better services or products, so too do citizen and business choices incentivize governments to perform better.[57] The results of this stimulus will include responsiveness to preferences, innovation in policy offerings, and efficient use of public resources.

Arguments supporting the beneficial effects of interstate competition hold the most water with economic development policy—states have a vested interest in making sure their policies on infrastructure, job training, land use, early childhood and K–12 education, and business incentives (loan and grant programs; tax breaks) are attractive to businesses and citizens. With regard to policies concerning ideological issues, interstate variation makes sense as well. Because there are strong beliefs on both sides of the debate over abortion and gay marriage, for instance, federalism and the policy variation it enables are attractive features of American government.

But what about social policy? Do these arguments hold up in this policy arena as well? Responsiveness, innovation, and efficiency sound appealing, and are certainly far nobler motives for state control than the racism that shaped the origins of many means-tested programs. But how do these arguments stand up to Marcella and Dave's experiences—and those of millions of other recipients of means-tested programs?

Responsiveness

One rationale for state (and local) control of social assistance programs is that states are closer to the people than the federal government 'way off in Washington, DC, and can therefore better assess needs and tailor policies to local conditions. This perspective holds that local discretion and autonomy are desirable in order to meet people's needs in such a large, diverse nation. Naturally, social provision will vary, because conditions on the ground vary—that's the essence of responsiveness.

If this effect actually materialized—if states responded to need—

then more generous programs and more spending would occur where and when poverty is greater. In reality, the exact opposite patterns emerge. Poor states do the least to help their poor residents, not the most. And during economic downturns, states often reduce rather than increase spending on means-tested programs, just when the need is greatest.

Across states, a *negative* relationship exists between need and social assistance provision that undercuts the responsiveness argument. Poor states spend less (as do conservative states).[58] Medicaid's federal match formula is one program feature that tries to level these differences in state wealth and fiscal capacity, but it falls short: poor states still lag in Medicaid effort. One problem is that the per capita income measure used in the formula is more loosely correlated with actual Medicaid need than some alternatives are, such as the poverty rate or personal income per poor person.[59] For example, New York and Massachusetts have the same per capita income, and so get the same Medicaid match, but the New York poverty rate is 60 percent higher. Similarly, Mississippi, Louisiana, and New Mexico have higher poverty rates than other low-income states, but don't get a greater match.[60] The match formula also ignores differential needs created by variations in target populations across states. For example, the Medicaid population in a given state could be disproportionately young and therefore inexpensive to care for in Medicaid, or they could be disproportionately older, with many chronic conditions and long-term care needs and therefore more expensive to cover. But the formula doesn't take these demographic differences into account.[61]

Responsiveness is weak not only across states but also over time. During economic downturns, the need for social assistance increases as people lose jobs and income. Yet because states lose revenue during these periods and because nearly every state must balance its budget each year, they often cut nonmandatory social assistance programs during recessions rather than expand them. For example, during the Great Recession that began in 2007, Arizona not only closed off CHIP enrollment to new children but also reduced the time limit for TANF from sixty months to thirty-six. Massachusetts cut adult dental care in its Medicaid program, as noted earlier. The State of Washington reduced cash grants in its Disability Lifeline program for the physically and mentally disabled. Pennsylvania reduced its state SSI supplement. Mississippi slashed its mental health budget. South Carolina reduced Medicaid hospital payments by 7 percent and physicians' reimbursements by 10 percent.[62] The list of social assistance cuts goes on and on.[63] Such reductions reinforce downturns, making recessions even worse, whereas policy responsiveness would dictate greater, countercyclical spending to meet increased need.[64]

The fact that Marcella and Dave would have a completely different public policy experience in different states, despite being the same people with the same needs, undercuts the responsiveness argument for state control.[65] Public policy can hardly be called responsive when Marcella would receive more personal care hours in one state than another, or when she and Dave could have unlimited assets in one state but just $2,000 in assets in another. Or when Logan would be insured in most states but without health insurance in others. That the same people get different amounts of help depending on their location is the opposite of responsiveness. That some states can't do more for the poor (for fiscal reasons) or won't (for ideological reasons) results in variations in assistance that are difficult to justify in a country that holds opportunity and justice dear.

Innovation

Others argue that state control of public policy fosters innovation. Supreme Court associate justice Louis Brandeis famously called states "laboratories of democracy" that can experiment with policy designs. Successful innovations are then adopted by other states and possibly the federal government as well.

Certainly, many innovations have proved successful and have been adopted more widely. Many states have engaged in Medicaid experimentation, such as allotting long-term care dollars for home health care, which most people prefer to nursing home care. During CHIP's early years, states quickly adopted policies shown by others to lower children's uninsurance rates.[66] The Massachusetts health reform of

2006 became the template for the national Affordable Care Act of 2010. New Jersey first experimented with diagnostic-related groups, a hospital payment system later adopted by Medicare. Many advocates currently urge the wider adoption of the paid family and medical leave policies that California and New Jersey pioneered. Creative, effective ideas proved in one state can then be taken up by others.

One downside of innovation is that it can turn sour. For example, in criminal justice policy, prison privatization lowers costs for state and local governments, but also lowers quality: prisons run by private contractors suffer more understaffing, undertrained personnel, and violence than government-run correctional facilities.[67] Innovations can fall short in social policy as well. I'm sure that California thought it was doing SSI recipients a favor when it barred them from applying for food stamps and increased the state's SSI supplement instead. But as the size of the supplement has fallen behind the current value of food stamps, this "innovation" has effectively become a benefit reduction for recipients. Similarly, advocates of the disabled in Massachusetts are very concerned about a demonstration project enabled by the Affordable Care Act in which managed care organizations will get both Medicare and Medicaid dollars to provide medical insurance and long-term services and supports to dual eligibles— those disabled and elderly people qualifying for both programs. This is the first time that one entity has been given responsibility for both medical insurance *and* LTSS. The goal of the experiment is to provide better-coordinated care for this complex population, which has heretofore been divided across Medicare and Medicaid, and to save costs, which have been booming for home health care.[68] While agreeing with these goals, many advocates are worried that such organizations will have incentives to reduce personal care assistant hours and other services in a capitated payment scheme (where they get a set amount of money for each patient), and that even with the best of intentions the end result will be reduced services.[69]

Marcella and Dave have certainly benefited from innovations in California, such as the Access for Infants and Mothers insurance program for pregnant middle-income women and the paid family leave policy. But they have also suffered because of state policy sclerosis: the Medi-Cal asset test level hasn't been adjusted since 1989 and is now worth half as much in real terms; stagnant wages make it hard to find personal care assistants beyond family members. Innovation is desirable but uneven, across states, across time, and across programs, to the detriment of program beneficiaries.

Efficiency

In public policy, efficiency means increased or improved outputs for identical or decreased input.[70] That individuals and businesses can leave the state in which they reside is supposed to induce state governments to optimize their performance and provide residents with the most value for their tax dollars.

However, when it comes to social assistance, it's not at all clear that interstate competition produces efficient outcomes. Instead, it may simply induce states to develop less redistributive policy in order to keep taxes low,[71] providing savings today but greater costs tomorrow, or creating savings in one arena but greater expense in another.

For example, low Medicaid provider payments save money in the short run, but could result in substantial costs for states if recipients can't find providers who will accept them and instead forego treatment or resort to hospital emergency rooms for primary care. In Kentucky, which hadn't raised its Medicaid payments in ten years, the president-elect of the state medical association said in reference to Medicaid patients who can't find a primary care physician, "There's no question that for some patients, emergency rooms have become the main method of care." In his own practice, he cut the proportion of Medicaid patients from 25 to 15 percent. "The type of insurance a person has shouldn't be a factor in patient care. But it's difficult to run a practice if you aren't getting reimbursed."[72] Overall, states that spend less on Medicaid end up with worse health care access and worse health outcomes.[73]

California's Medi-Cal is a particularly low payer. Its reimbursements to physicians and hospitals as a proportion of Medicare fees are very low compared with other states; its spending per Medicaid child was just two-thirds of the national average in 2009.[74] While the low payments might seem like a good deal for the state, they're problematic for Medi-Cal beneficiaries, who can have a difficult time finding physicians willing to take them on as patients. Marcella has regular appointments with her rehabilitation and physical medicine doctor, himself a quadriplegic who went to medical school after his injury, and a real source of inspiration and advice. But she has to wait a long time to see other specialists, and there's one she never was able to see to follow up on her vocal cord injury. Dave says, "As Medi-Cal patients, we're last on the wait list."

This short-term (and short-sighted) cost-shaving orientation can have more dangerous consequences. After leaving the rehab hospital, Marcella used a special cushioned mattress topper specifically designed to prevent the pressure sores that are so threatening to quadriplegics and so expensive to repair surgically. Four months later, Medi-Cal announced it would no longer pay for the high-quality topper. It gave her a flimsy replacement, because she "didn't have enough bed sores." Maybe next time she will, costing Medi-Cal far more.

Choice

What about the power of choice that undergirds the entire rationale for state policy control and interstate variation? Who actually can actively choose where they live, and with what implications for policy?

Many state policy makers think the poor have a choice, and so they refuse to offer generous social assistance benefits for fear of becoming a "welfare magnet." While empirical examinations of the welfare magnet phenomenon are inconclusive, what matters is that state lawmakers think the effect exists, and make policy accordingly.[75]

But in fact, for many the choice of location is an illusion. An important study of poor single mothers found that while the generosity of welfare benefits did influence state residential choice somewhat, many move back to their home state, where their family network and connections are.[76] The same considerations hold for Dave and

Marcella. Thinking solely about their finances, they should probably move from California to a state without a Medicaid asset test. Then Marcella could get the health coverage she needs without the family being denied financial security. Or they should move to Massachusetts, which has better provisions for the disabled, not to mention some of the best hospitals and top doctors in the nation for Marcella. But they're not going to move. Dave has lived his entire life in Redding. Marcella's whole family lives there. Sure, the social policy situation might be better elsewhere, but where else would a large and dedicated group of friends have rebuilt their house for them? No state will pay for wheelchair renovations. Where else would Marcella have a team of family members who share in providing her personal care? No state will pay for twenty-four-hour coverage. Dave and Marcella have no "choice." They have to remain where they have access to the crucial network of family and lifelong friends that provides the supports they need for her profound needs—needs that are covered incompletely even in the most generous states.

When it comes to social assistance, the outcomes of responsiveness, innovation, and efficiency promised by state control and policy variation don't always emerge. Indeed, competition among states can induce worse outcomes rather than better ones in this arena. And choice is elusive for many low-income people, leaving them mired in locations where they can't get sufficient help.

INCREASING THE CENTRALIZATION OF SOCIAL ASSISTANCE

As Dave and Marcella's experience shows, it's difficult to justify the tremendous variation in means-tested programs across states. As the next chapter discusses, in other countries subnational governments often administer social programs and perform needs assessments, as in the United States. However, the United States is unusual in allowing states to define who gets what—the actual content of policies—and in imposing on states a degree of financial responsibility that results in widely varying levels of assistance. Such vast differences simply don't exist to the same degree in other economically advanced nations.

Yet even in the United States, a national interest in social assistance becoming both more comprehensive and more consistent is on the rise. For example, most Americans will eventually be eligible for Medicare, a federal program. If some of them are in poorer health by the time they reach the age of sixty-five because they were uninsured as adults due to state policy (such as narrow Medicaid eligibility), then the national program is worse off: those people will end up being more costly than healthier individuals from a state that provides more expansive social assistance. Beyond these pragmatic matters is the fact that the national government is supposed to promote "the general welfare." Dramatic cross-state differences in public policy arguably conflict with this tenet of American citizenship.[77]

Changes in social assistance over the last thirty years have increased the federal role, and suggest an at least tacit recognition that state variation in this area is neither effective nor desirable. In two primarily federal programs, the EITC and food stamps, benefit levels and eligibility have gradually expanded, partly offsetting state variation and decline in other means-tested programs.

In two joint federal-state programs, Medicaid and CHIP, eligibility has expanded as well, due to provisions emanating from the federal side. Congress has repeatedly added new groups to the list of populations that state Medicaid programs must cover, particularly during the 1980s and 1990s. The Affordable Care Act incentivizes states to further increase Medicaid eligibility to all persons below 138 percent of the poverty level (not just poor children and pregnant women) by paying 100 percent of the costs for the newly eligible (eventually declining to 90 percent, but still higher than the usual Medicaid match).

A greater federal role is evidenced in CHIP as well. The program has a higher federal match than Medicaid does, to encourage states to cover as many low-income children as possible. Furthermore, when it was reauthorized in 2009, funding was increased substantially by raising the federal tobacco tax. The reauthorization also included provisions intended to maximize enrollment: states must use their allotted CHIP funds within a certain period or lose them, and they receive annual performance bonuses for exceeding their enrollment targets.[78]

In all these social assistance programs there has been increased "centralization," with the federal government both expanding enrollment and/or benefits and helping to pay the new costs.[79] The infusion of new dollars and enhanced eligibility rules helps decrease state variation.

That said, much of the new federal help has been aimed at jobholders rather than nonworkers. The EITC and CHIP both explicitly target the working poor. Expansions in Medicaid and food stamps have brought more low-wage workers into those programs as well. At the same time, programs that substantially benefit nonworkers, such as TANF and public housing, have been static or shrinking, and there has been no move to enhance the federal role. Thus, while social protections for low-income workers have in some ways become more robust, social assistance for nonworkers remains a policy backwater of low funding and pronounced cross-state variation.

HOW YOU FARE DEPENDS ON WHERE YOU SIT

States make their own laws in a variety of areas: that's the way American federalism works. In turn, citizens—at least the mobile ones—can choose to live where policies correspond to their preferences. Firms too can locate where conditions best suit their business needs. Variation and competition among states are supposed to induce an upward spiral of policy responsiveness, innovation, and efficiency, and perhaps do accomplish these objectives in certain policy arenas.

When it comes to social assistance, however, state variation is problematic. It's easy to see where such inequality comes from: low-income states can afford to do less for the poor than states with richer citizens and greater tax capacity. Ideology plays a role as well, albeit a lesser one, with conservative states having less generous programs than more liberal states. But variation in social assistance across states is hard to defend, either economically or morally.

Economically, state variation in means-tested social policy imposes real costs. The amount of state effort in health insurance, cash assistance, housing, education, and other supports has major impacts on a variety of outcomes, including citizen health, educational attainment, financial security, and productivity. Where state efforts fall short, the federal government ultimately picks up the tab—in higher Medicare expenditures for the unhealthy, or in higher SSI payments to the destitute, to mention just a couple of adverse outcomes. Recognition of the federal stake in means-tested programs, and the need to equalize effort across states with differing levels of wealth and tax capacity, is evidenced in a couple of ways: the Medicaid match formula, which provides more federal dollars to poorer states; the expansion in recent years of federally funded means-tested programs (CHIP, food stamps, EITC). But state variation remains. Spending patterns are neither responsive nor efficient, despite hopes that they would be. Innovation and choice are oversold. And where state efforts fall short, real people suffer real consequences.

Morally, it's difficult to say that the same poor person should have health insurance in Minnesota but not in Texas. Or that the same disabled person should have ten hours of personal care per day in North Dakota but none at all in Tennessee, just a few years ago. Americans are citizens of the nation, yet the meaning of that citizenship varies tremendously depending on where they live within the country. Americans are treated less equally than the citizens of virtually any advanced democracy, as we'll see in the next chapter. On what principle could that variation be justified?

CONCLUSION THE FUTURE OF AMERICAN MEANS-TESTED PROGRAMS

By May 2013, fifteen months after the accident, Marcella and Dave had settled into a routine, although still a temporary one. Marcella was attending physical therapy sessions three or four days per week. Dave was back at work—and finally went to a doctor. Amazingly, his blood pressure was fine. The doctor just urged him to return to his usual exercise routine. Logan's teeth came in, and he learned to crawl and then to walk and run with increasing steadiness and speed. A highlight for the whole family was National Nurses Day, when Marcella returned to Mercy Medical Center in Redding to speak with the nurses, doctors, and EMTs who had helped her in the weeks after the accident. She wanted to "use this whole thing to do a little good" and let the medical staff know what a huge impact they have on patients. Meanwhile, Logan charmed all present, running around and giving out hugs.

Marcella and Dave had not yet moved back into their home. With volunteer labor from an extraordinary group of friends, the renovation to make the house wheelchair accessible was under way. But the project was slow going. On several occasions, the crew ran out of money for materials that hadn't been donated outright, but every time some angel came through. By December 2013, happily, the flooring was down, the plumbing was in, and the lights were on, and we were able to open Christmas gifts in Marcella and Dave's reconfigured kitchen/living room, a big boost to their spirits. They hoped to move back in early spring 2014, which would help a lot—they and Logan each had been staying with different relatives, and were long overdue to live as a family under one roof.

Mom had returned home in May 2013, a moment I had been dreading. She loved bonding with Logan and helping Dave and Marcella during this tumultuous period. But she had put her entire life on hold for fifteen months, sleeping on a sofa bed and living out of a suitcase. She needed to get back to her own routine, not to mention the fact that an increasingly active and curious toddler was becoming quite a handful for a woman of seventy-eight. At first it wasn't clear who would take care of Logan when she left. Then a preschool in town offered to take him "on scholarship." The director worked with Marcella to secure funding that pays most of the cost. Marcella says the money came from a program that "helps pay for child care for welfare families," so it's likely Community Block Development Grant money or something along those lines.[1] Logan had risen to the top of the waiting list because of her disability.

As for Logan's opinion of the preschool, he loves it. On days when he's sick and has to stay home, he pounds on the front door, begging to be driven there. The adults in his life are utterly relieved that he has a place to go while Dave is at work—and thrilled that it is such a high-quality, enriching center as well.

But many questions about the family's future remain. It appears that Marcella and Dave will have to stay on Medi-Cal forever. Is there *any* path back to the middle class? This chapter lays out their options, each grimmer than the next, it seems. It then moves beyond Dave and Marcella's situation to discuss the ways in which the American system of social protections—or lack thereof—is unique among advanced-economy nations. Nowhere among other rich nations do the poor experience quite the marginalization, lack of support, and geographic variation that exist in the United States. And it could get worse: the future of means-tested programs in this fiscally challenged era is considered at the end of the chapter. Will American social policies change to better meet the needs of the nation's people, or will budgetary and ideological battles render them even less complete?

CAN MARCELLA AND DAVE EVER ESCAPE MEDI-CAL?

We are profoundly grateful in many ways. There is a safety net. For the most part, Marcella is receiving the medical care that she needs. Surrounded by middle-class family members, she and Dave are much better off than the truly poor.

Researchers have studied how the very impoverished actually live, given that social assistance is so meager: pooling and swapping their limited goods; relying on informal caregivers for their children; combining households and living in crowded conditions; selling goods on the black market.[2] For some, the situation is truly bleak. In Detroit, the extremely poor live in condemned houses, selling their food stamps for half the face value to pay utility bills, and trapping rabbits, raccoons, and in the winter, rats and mice, for food.[3]

Dave and Marcella are a long way from eating rats. But they are desperate to escape Medi-Cal's financial restrictions. They would love to have the safety of savings; they don't want to raise their son with so much insecurity and uncertainty. Is there any way for them to leave Medi-Cal's income and asset limits behind and return to a middle-class lifestyle?

Medicare

What about Medicare? What about swapping the lower tier of social assistance for the upper tier of social insurance, where recipients can get public health insurance without an income or asset test, leaving their life of penury behind?

After all, Medicare is the public health insurance program that's for not just older Americans but also the permanently disabled. It isn't means-tested. A person doesn't have to be poor to receive it. On Medicare, Dave and Marcella could earn any amount of money without penalty. They could have assets, accept financial help from family members, and raise their son in the manner they intended.

Sounds good. Except for a prohibitive set of problems, as the reader knows by now.

Problem #1: Medicare covers the permanently disabled only after a two-year waiting period. What would Marcella do for insurance in the interim? She'd probably go on Medi-Cal. Perhaps after 2014, the Affordable Care Act's ban on insurers' ability to deny coverage to those with preexisting medical conditions would allow a newly disabled person to purchase private insurance, but that certainly wasn't the case in 2012. The waiting period thwarts escape from social assistance.

Problem #2: Medicare is not very complete insurance. With a hospital stay, Marcella would be subject to the $1,184 deductible for each episode of illness plus coinsurance of $296 per day for days 61 to 90 and $592 per day for days 91 to 150. Considering that she will likely face many hospitalizations over her lifetime because quadriplegics have a lot of system complications, these out-of-pocket costs could really add up. For Medicare Part B, which covers doctors' visits, Marcella would have to pay an annual deductible of $147 and a $104.90 monthly premium (2013 figures). She would also owe 20 percent coinsurance for doctors' visits and services and for any Medicare-covered medical equipment. For prescription drugs, she would have to pay an additional monthly premium, and perhaps deductibles and co-payments for these drugs as well. Unlike a senior citizen subject to the same cost-sharing, Marcella as a disabled person isn't allowed to purchase a medigap plan to cover these expenses. So she'd probably have to go on Medi-Cal for the wraparound coverage. Again, so much for escaping social assistance.

Moreover, and crucially, Medicare doesn't cover the long-term services and supports that disabled people need, such as personal care assistance. Long-term care was intentionally left out of Medicare from its inception—feared as a budget buster.[4] The only public program providing such care is Medicaid/Medi-Cal. If you need LTSS, you can't leave social assistance.

Problem #3: For Marcella, all the above are moot: she isn't eligible for Medicare. Because she is young, and had gone back to school at the time of the accident, she hadn't worked enough quarters to qualify. If you aren't a worker, an *insured* worker, you are relegated to the means-tested tier.

So Medicare provides no exit.

Private Insurance and the Affordable Care Act

Perhaps Marcella and Dave could get private health insurance, through either a new job for Dave or the health insurance exchanges of the Obama administration's health reform, the Patient Protection and Affordable Care Act of 2010 (ACA). However, it isn't clear that they'd be better off in private insurance than under Medi-Cal. Before getting to their case, it's worth reviewing what the ACA does and doesn't do to change the contours of health insurance in the United States.

In March 2010, president Barack Obama signed the Patient Protection and Affordable Care Act, a historic achievement after decades of unsuccessful attempts to reform the American health insurance system. The ACA is not national health insurance; millions of Americans will remain uninsured even after it is fully implemented. But it begins to address some of the worst consequences of the prereform situation.

The ACA has two main parts. As written, the "Affordable Care" component requires most Americans to have health insurance (the individual mandate). It enables them to do so by expanding Medicaid to all citizens under 138 percent of the federal poverty level (later altered by the Supreme Court); requiring employers above a certain size to offer health insurance (the employer mandate); and creating "health exchanges" or "marketplaces" on which the remaining uninsured individuals and small businesses such as Dave's can buy insurance at group rates, with a sliding scale of subsidies for individuals with incomes between 100 and 400 percent of the federal poverty level. Small businesses that offer health insurance receive tax breaks.

The "Patient Protection" part of the law seeks to curb many of the practices of private insurers that limit coverage. These new regulations are important, because private insurers continue to play a large role postreform: individuals currently with private insurance through their employer keep their arrangements intact, and the law uses private insurance to expand coverage (the health exchange options will be private plans, and most Medicaid enrollees are in private managed care plans as well). As of January 2014, insurers can no longer deny coverage for preexisting conditions—that is, they can no longer refuse to offer insurance to customers having a prior medical condition. Nor can they impose annual or lifetime caps on health coverage (no more limits on the benefits they will pay out) or rescind coverage except in cases of fraud. They also must spend a certain proportion of premiums on health care (rather than on administration or other nonclinical functions). Moreover, insurers are required to submit premium increases for review by state insurance regulators.[5]

Thus, the ACA takes aim at some of the worst problems in the pre-existing health insurance system. When fully implemented, it will significantly reduce the uninsured population. Insurance expansion will come about in part because new populations will be eligible for Medicaid,[6] and those previously eligible but unenrolled may step forward in response to publicity and outreach efforts emanating from the reform. Still others will have coverage newly offered by their employers, and others will be able to buy insurance on a health exchange. Americans previously denied insurance because of preexisting medical conditions will now be able to get insurance. The ACA improves preventive health and mental health coverage as well.

The expansion of the health insurance umbrella should have a number of positive effects. Having health insurance coverage increases both a person's financial security and his or her use of medical services.[7] By covering more people, the reform partly addresses the problem that the uninsured receive less medical care than the insured do. The ACA's combination of the employer mandate, the availability of exchanges, and the ban on coverage prohibitions based on preexisting conditions should help relieve "job lock"—the phenomenon in which individuals feel tethered to a job for fear of losing health insurance. It is also an enormous help to several groups with high uninsurance rates: the young, who often go without insurance between school and a job with an affordable plan; the self-employed, who faced aggressive medical underwriting and high premiums on the old individual insurance market; and those who retire early, by choice or by force, but are too young for Medicare coverage. In addition to addressing problems among the uninsured, the ACA also should relieve some of the difficulties of the underinsured. Medical-related financial distress and bankruptcy should decline with the law's elimination of insurers' annual and lifetime limits on benefits.

The legislation will do much to improve the health insurance situation of many people, both expanding access and increasing the quality of health insurance plans. It does have its shortcomings, though. It doesn't extend health insurance to everyone. Some groups are exempted from the individual mandate to have insurance: those whose incomes fall below the tax-filing threshold; Native Americans; incarcerated individuals; and those with financial hardship. Illegal immigrants are both exempted from the mandate and prohibited from buying insurance on an exchange, even with their own money. Most significantly, millions more will receive no assistance for health insurance coverage, as they are ineligible for either Medicaid or subsidies to buy private insurance on the exchanges.

The Supreme Court ruled in June 2012 that the Medicaid expansion is optional for states, and as a result about half the states—home to more than half the nation's uninsured—initially announced they would not broaden Medicaid eligibility.[8] Many of those states may change course and expand Medicaid in the future. In the meantime, however, the problem is that poor individuals in the states that don't expand are also ineligible for subsidies on the exchanges, because Congress had assumed in the ACA that they'd be covered by Medicaid.[9] Consequently, in states that don't expand Medicaid, people below the poverty line who try to sign up for health insurance will be told they are ineligible for assistance; if they made just a little more money, then they could get subsidized coverage on an exchange. As one child advocate said, "In states that do not expand Medicaid, some of the neediest people will not get coverage. But people who are just above the poverty line or in the middle class can get subsidized coverage. People will be denied assistance because they don't make enough money. Trying to explain that will be a nightmare."[10]

A January 2013 ruling by the IRS also undercut coverage expansion for the spouses and children of some workers. As written by Congress, the ACA states that people who have access to "affordable" insurance through their employer cannot get subsidies to buy health insurance on the exchanges instead (the intent was to prevent people from leaving employer-provided coverage for the exchanges). The ACA defines "affordable" coverage as costing no more than 9.5 percent of family income. But the IRS ruling tied "affordability" to the cost of health coverage for an *individual* worker, typically around $5,600, not the cost of family coverage, which costs about three times as much, around $15,700. Therefore, if an employer is unwilling to pay a portion of family premiums, some family members may remain uninsured, unable to afford the full premium on their own and ineligible for the subsidies.[11]

Under the ACA, people with large swings in income from year to year may be confused as their eligibility for Medicaid versus exchange insurance plans shifts, or as the size of their insurance subsidies changes. There are concerns about continuity of care for those who churn across Medicaid and exchange eligibility thresholds—will they have to switch doctors, for example.[12] On the other hand, before the ACA, such churning was in and out of health insurance altogether, so the law represents a considerable improvement.

Variation across states in terms of health insurance eligibility and benefits also continues under the ACA, particularly in Medicaid. As noted, about half the states are expanding the program, while half are not. Thus, a below-poverty childless adult is eligible for Medicaid in one state but not another. Aspects of the marketplaces vary as well. Individuals shopping on the exchanges can choose from one or two health plans in some states but from among ten or more in others.[13] Fourteen states have their own health exchanges, while most are instead using exchanges run by the federal government (the federal portal was famously nonfunctional during its early months). States also vary in the rigorousness of their regulatory practices, for example in how they review and react to proposed insurance premium increases.[14] On the other hand, the ACA does provide uniformity apart from Medicaid: all states have an insurance marketplace, and the subsidy schedule for those between 100 and 400 percent of the poverty level is the same nationwide. And in those states expanding Medicaid, rules for the newly eligible are much more straightforward than the Byzantine rules that had accrued for the older eligibility groups.

Will the Affordable Care Act Help Dave and Marcella?

The ACA will give millions of Americans access to health insurance, and will improve the insurance coverage of millions more. But will it help Dave and Marcella? Unfortunately, that seems unlikely. Although the law improves things for many, including substantial portions of the diverse disabled community, it doesn't help everyone. Particularly for the permanently and severely physically disabled like Marcella who need personal care assistance, the ACA doesn't much change the status quo.

The ACA certainly may help Dave. It's unlikely that his current employer will begin to offer health insurance. The company is too small to come under the employer mandate. Despite the tax breaks it would receive if it offered health insurance, that's still an extra expense for a business operating on a slim margin. As of 2014, Dave can purchase private insurance for himself on a health insurance exchange in California (if he returned to his pre-accident income, he would be ineligible for Medi-Cal, although Logan would still be eligible). A quick look on California's health exchange website, Covered California, revealed that his 2014 monthly premium is $105 for a Bronze plan, for which he'd be responsible for 60 percent of his health care costs on average, or $194 for an "Enhanced Silver 87 plan," for which he'd be responsible for 13 percent of health care costs.[15]

Whether the ACA helps Marcella is another question. In theory, she could leave Medi-Cal for private insurance purchased on a health exchange: the ACA bans insurers from denying coverage to people with preexisting medical conditions; it removes annual and lifetime limits on medical claims; and it offers insurers reinsurance for large claims. In the pre-ACA world, very few disabled people could buy individual insurance because of their expensive risk profiles. No insurer would accept them—of the 7,000 adults under the age of sixty-five with serious chronic health conditions or disabilities included in the 30,000-person 2004 Medical Expenditure Panel Survey, only 13 had individually purchased insurance.[16] With the ACA eliminating medical underwriting of this type and giving individuals access to group rates on the health exchanges, Marcella could theoretically qualify for a private plan.[17]

Yet private health insurance poses the same dilemma as Medicare: it doesn't cover the LTSS disabled people need, such as personal care assistants. The ACA once contained a voluntary social insurance program for long-term care called Community Living Assistance Services and Supports. Workers could elect to pay into the system, and after a five-year vesting period would be eligible for a daily LTC allowance with no lifetime limit. However, because the CLASS program was voluntary, and therefore subject to adverse selection—those most likely to need LTC would have been most likely to sign up—in October 2011, the secretary of the Department of Health and Human Services deemed the program fiscally unsustainable and declined to implement it. The American Taxpayer Relief Act of 2012 (the "fiscal cliff" bill) officially repealed CLASS.[18]

And so Medicaid remains the only public program providing LTSS. Private LTC insurance has time limits and is of little use to the permanently disabled (plus it can't be purchased after disability occurs).[19] The ACA does nothing to change these basic facts. The law is about expanding coverage and minimizing the worst problems with private health insurance, not about disability. It leaves a lot of issues for the severely disabled on the table. It also retains the basic boundaries between employer-provided insurance, Medicare, and Medicaid to minimize the opposition that had defeated previous efforts to reform American health care.[20] But in doing so, the ACA does little to alter the reality that a poverty program is virtually the only way for the severely disabled to get the care they need. It does nothing to alleviate the "extreme choice" the disabled face between claiming their disability or relinquishing that claim in order to work but giving up the supports they require. For the many Americans who will be newly—and better—insured, the ACA is a godsend. Given Marcella's need for LTSS, it's virtually irrelevant to her and Dave's situation.[21]

In one regard, the ACA made Marcella worse off. As a budgetary measure in response to the law's expansion of Medicaid, the California legislature decided to require Medi-Cal recipients in rural counties to transition from their existing fee-for-service arrangements (where physicians and hospitals are paid for each episode of care) into managed care plans.[22] The problem is that rural counties typically have few if any managed care plans in place. Marcella received a letter in the fall of 2013 telling her that if her current primary care physician wasn't participating in the new managed care system (Dr. S was not), she had to select a new physician from a provided list. In the enclosure, only two options were listed: the local public health clinic, which was taking new patients, or a family practice clinic run by medical residents at Mercy Medical Center, which was not. Marcella really didn't want to go to the public health clinic, which is the county's last-resort safety-net provider,[23] and so her mother managed to persuade the Mercy family practice clinic to accept her as a patient. Marcella can continue to see the same specialists with a referral, but her primary care physician these days is a medical resident, a doctor-in-training who may never have had a quadriplegic patient before, and who will turn over every three years.[24]

Litigation

In his informative and provocative 2007 book, *The Welfare State Nobody Knows*, Chris Howard shows that the American welfare state is far larger than it appears if we include all the ways in which social protections are provided besides direct-spending programs: tax expenditures and delegation to private entities such as employers (discussed in this book); use of quasi-governmental entities such as Sallie Mae and Freddie Mac (which facilitate higher education and home ownership, respectively, through reduced interest rates); and litigation. When I first read the book, I did a double take. Litigation— suing in court to win a monetary settlement—isn't social policy, I thought. It's not systematic. Its outcomes depend on the details of the case, the skill of the lawyers, the makeup of the jury. Howard's argument seemed ridiculous.

Now I know what he meant, as the scales fall from my eyes post-accident. In the absence of effective social policy to help them, some try the courtroom crapshoot. Marcella and Dave might join the gamblers and sue to get money for her care.

Sue whom? The driver of the other vehicle was never found. Go after the car manufacturer? And then there's the other problem with litigation: could it actually yield a large-enough settlement to facilitate a departure from Medi-Cal? That seems unlikely: Marcella would have to win millions of dollars to ensure she'd have enough for her LTSS and living expenses for decades into the future. More commonly, disabled people stay on Medicaid, and any money they win in a lawsuit is put into a special-needs trust, which carries very specific rules that vary by state: in order not to threaten Medicaid eligibility, the trust can't be used for any purposes for which the disabled person is reliant on means-tested programs. That is, in California the trust money can't be used for everyday living expenses, health coverage, or home health care. It can be used only for "extras," like a family vacation. Don't get me wrong—a vacation at some accessible resort would be a very welcome change of pace for Dave and Marcella—but such a trust would do little to relieve the everyday limitations of their living under Medi-Cal's financial constraints. And that's if they even won the lawsuit. Litigation is clearly not much of an answer to Dave and Marcella's difficulties.

Divorce

The options thus far aren't too promising. Neither Medicare nor private insurance offers Marcella a path away from Medi-Cal. Litigation is probably a pipe dream. There's one thing Dave could do to get out from under Marcella's Medi-Cal restrictions: divorce her. This would separate Marcella and Dave's income and assets. Only Marcella would then be forced into impoverishment; Dave could keep his half of the assets. And he and Logan would be free to live on as much income as Dave could make, to accept help from family members, to establish a 529 college fund, to have emergency money put away, to save for Dave's retirement. In other words, they could go back to their middle-class life. And unattached to a spouse, Marcella would be eligible for means-tested programs without the "deeming rules" that count a spouse's income and assets.

Such "Medicaid divorces" are common among the elderly. When one member of a couple becomes disabled and needs to move to a nursing home, the couple divorces to separate their assets. Then the disabled former partner "spends down" his or her assets on nursing home fees until the state's asset limit is reached, and then goes on Medicaid. In this manner, some assets for the spouse remaining in the community are protected.[25]

Of course, getting divorced at the age of eighty-five from your spouse of many decades is awful. Now imagine that you're half that age, you've been married only three years, you intended to spend the rest of your lives together. And you have a young son whom you wish to raise together. Are you really going to get divorced? And yet that appears to be the wisest path under current American social policy.

A Ray of Hope? The California Working Disabled Program

Perhaps there is one good option for Dave and Marcella. In 2000, California created the Medi-Cal California Working Disabled Program. This program is meant to encourage the disabled to work without threatening their Medi-Cal eligibility.[26] It is a Medi-Cal buy-in program aimed directly at the stark choice Medicaid enrollees usually face: stay on Medicaid forever, or relinquish their public insurance in order to get a job. Under the CWD program, as long as disabled enrollees work at least a few hours every month, they can buy into Medi-Cal with a sliding-scale monthly premium payment rather than have to enroll in Medi-Cal through the more expensive Share of Cost program (monthly premiums range from $20 to $250 for individuals).[27] To be eligible, enrollees must meet the Social Security definition of disability, earn less than 250 percent of the federal poverty line, and meet Medi-Cal's asset limit.

I first learned of CWD in an e-mail that a disability law attorney sent me after Marcella's accident. The more I researched the program, the more promising it seemed. With CWD, Dave and Marcella would still be subject to the Medi-Cal asset test, but they could live on a much higher income. Their potential retained income could essentially double, to 250 percent of the poverty level.[28] Even better than that: Marcella's SSI benefits aren't included in their "countable income," the income they're allowed to live on.[29] Moreover, under CWD rules, Marcella can have an employer or individual retirement plan such as an IRA or 401(k); these kinds of retirement funds aren't counted as assets for this program. Thus, she could put away her earnings in an IRA, and the couple could have a little more income in retirement. Yet another recent change makes CWD even more attractive: new program rules now allow the disabled worker to save earnings in a separate bank account, the value of which is not limited and does not count against the program's asset limit.[30] So Dave and Marcella could put away her earnings and establish an emergency fund.

The more I read about the program from State of California websites and heard from policy experts, the better the option seemed. Marcella would still need to remain on Medi-Cal to get the health insurance and LTSS she needs, but she and Dave could return to their pre-accident income level—and more. In addition, they could establish an emergency fund and even an IRA with her earnings. And her health insurance would cost at most $250 per month.

I e-mailed this information to Dave. He responded, "Marce already spoke to the Medi-Cal folk, and they said she was not eligible for the CWD program." He added, "Not exactly sure why; her regurgitation of the M-C person's denial left me with a question mark in my head, but the quick answer is that there is an uphill battle already there."

It seemed impossible that Marcella wasn't eligible for CWD. After all, it epitomized the movement in disability policy in recent years toward incentivizing work. At first I thought the denial was simply caused by a local social worker's not being very familiar with the program. Marcella was transferred to several different people when she called about CWD; none of them seemed to know much about it, which suggested that this might be the case. Lack of familiarity would be understandable: only 8,200 out of Medi-Cal's 8 million beneficiaries are enrolled in CWD.

But sure enough, in consulting with state-level Medi-Cal officials, I discovered that Marcella is in fact ineligible for CWD. Why? Because she's currently in zero-cost Medi-Cal, and state and county officials are prohibited from making her "worse off," that is, making her pay a monthly premium for something she currently gets for free. If she wants to enter CWD, she would have to go before an administrative law judge and argue that she *does* want to pay a premium, and that she has good reason for needing to exceed the usual asset limits. Arguments that people have used in the past: for their new occupation, they want to be able to save up for a new computer and assistive technologies, which will cost more than the asset test will allow; they have an IRA from an earlier job and don't want it subjected to the asset test. I don't know whether the kind of argument Marcella would make—we want to make more money so our son doesn't have to grow up in poverty—would get a sympathetic hearing. But she and Dave have every incentive to pursue the CWD option. It appears to be the one path by which they can achieve a comfortable income and a modicum of savings.[31] But they'll have to fight their way in.

WHAT WOULD HELP?

Short of the CWD program, which remains a question mark, Marcella and Dave don't have a lot of great choices going forward. It seems likely they'll have to continue to live in financial peril for her to get the health insurance and personal care assistance she needs.

On the health insurance front, it would be far better for Marcella if our nation had a truly universal program in which everyone has equal access to health care. If universal health insurance were a reality in the United States, Marcella could see any provider and wouldn't be turned away because she is in low-pay welfare medicine. The ACA does try mightily to bridge the gaps between the different insurance systems. It makes Medicaid more like Medicare by raising Medicaid payments to primary care physicians to Medicare levels (although only for 2013 and 2014). It makes Medicare more like private insurance by covering annual checkups and by closing the Medicare prescription "doughnut hole"—the gap in the standard Medicare drug plan where insurance drops out and seniors have to pay 100 percent of their drug costs.[32] It makes private insurance more like Medicare by banning annual and lifetime limits on insurance coverage. Nonetheless, it keeps the basic divisions in place, and people in the lowest tier, like Marcella, get so frequently turned away.

On the LTSS front, Marcella would be far better off if LTC were provided on a universal rather than a social assistance basis—if she didn't have to be poor to get personal care. Indeed, the lack of universally provided LTC is a threat both to the nonelderly disabled like Marcella and to those who will become disabled later in life—which is most of us. At the age of sixty-five, the likelihood of needing home health care at some point in one's remaining years is 72 percent; the likelihood of needing nursing home care is 49 percent.[33] As disability law expert Sam Bagenstos notes, "If we live long enough, we're all going to have disabilities. That's one of the things about the disability community. We're all going to be a part of it, if we're lucky."[34] And yet in the United States, the only way for us to get public help with these expensive needs is to spend down our assets to the poverty level and Medicaid eligibility.

CARING FOR THE DISABLED ABROAD

Other countries do better. Advanced-economy nations fall into three groups when it comes to public LTC policy.[35] The United States is in the bottom group, with means-tested provision only, along with England. In the middle are mixed systems that provide some services universally, others on a means-tested basis, in a variety of permutations; Scotland, Ireland, France, Austria, Italy, Canada, Australia, and New Zealand fall into this group. At the top are countries that provide universal coverage of both institutional and home-based personal care to all care-dependent individuals. These include countries with social LTC insurance, like Germany and the Netherlands; countries that finance universal LTC through general tax revenues, like Sweden, Norway, and Denmark; and countries that include LTC in their regular health system, like Belgium.

In Germany, Marcella would have a completely different experience than in the United States. In 1995, the country established a universal social insurance program for LTC. A payroll tax on employers and employees (much like the American Social Security tax) funds a monthly benefit based on level of disability, as determined by a medical review board. The benefit can either pay for institutional care or provide cash for home health care, going to formal care workers or to family members. These long-term services are universal, not means-tested, and so individuals don't have to impoverish themselves to get public help, as in the United States. The system is also weighted toward home-based care, which most people prefer and which costs less than nursing home care.[36] Under the German system, Marcella would qualify for long-term services as the spouse of an insured worker, and she and Dave wouldn't have to spend down to poverty to receive her needed services and supports.

Marcella would fare well in the other universal programs as well (the Netherlands, the Nordic countries, and Belgium). In each case, LTSS are provided to all people who need them, regardless of income or age (Japan and South Korea have social long-term care insurance too, but benefits are focused on the elderly).

In many of the mixed systems too, Marcella would be better off than in the United States. In most Canadian provinces, nursing home care is means-tested, but home care is provided universally to all disabled persons, which would be perfect for Dave and Marcella since she wants to live at home. A number of other countries in this mixed group have universal home-care benefits—everyone assessed as care-dependent receives them—but the amount of the public benefit is adjusted for income. That can leave users and their families with substantial out-of-pocket costs.

Nonetheless, that approach is superior to the one in the United States, where Marcella and millions of other disabled people are able to get public help with their LTC needs only by being poor. The United States took a step in the right direction with the CLASS legislation, but the program was doomed by its voluntary nature. Social insurance doesn't work if it isn't truly social.

The failure of the CLASS program for LTC has serious and wide-ranging consequences. Given that disability will eventually touch most individuals and most families, "financially, everyone in America is going to experience the pain of not having this program," Bagenstos says.[37] We have had spectacular success with social insurance in the United States. The Social Security system provides peace of mind for millions of workers: no matter what happens in their working lives, they'll have a public pension in retirement. Germans have similar peace of mind when it comes to disability: for a mere 1.95 percent payroll tax, divided between employers and employees, they can rest assured that they will have LTSS no matter what happens at what age.[38] It's tough enough to be disabled. Why do we insist in addition that people make the cruel bargain to stay poor forever to get the services they need?

THE DISTINCTIVE NATURE OF
THE AMERICAN WELFARE STATE

The differences in how the poor are treated compared with everyone else are much starker in the United States than in other rich nations. The issue is not that the American welfare state is so much smaller than that of other advanced industrialized democracies. It's not, when all the modes by which protections are delivered are added together: direct public spending (where the United States is near the bottom of the list of rich democracies, ranking twentieth), indirect public spending through the tax code, and private spending. Adding together all of these, plus the net effect of taxes, the United States ranks fifth in social spending among countries in the Organisation for Economic Co-operation and Development.[39]

However, as political scientist Julia Lynch has pointed out, the American welfare state is unusual in a number of respects, all of which we have observed in this examination of means-tested programs through the lens of my brother and sister-in-law's experience.[40]

Reliance on (Incomplete) Private Provision of Needed Protections

First on Lynch's list is the fact that the United States is unusually dependent on the private provision of social goods. While many countries have dual public and private markets, ours relies more on private provision, often promoted and subsidized by the government: private pensions, employer-provided health insurance, an almost entirely private market for child care, and so on. The problem with private provision is that it's not universal and usually favors upper-income households. In other advanced-economy countries, these social protections—and more—are provided to all citizens, not just workers whose employers happen to offer such benefits.

As noted earlier, this private system is eroding, with fewer employers providing coverage. Another difficulty with private provision is that it is extremely easy to fall through the cracks—between school and a job, or between jobs. A colleague of mine was left severely injured with a broken neck after a car accident. As he lay in the hospital, unsure whether he'd be permanently paralyzed, he and his wife found comfort in the fact that he'd just signed a contract for a new faculty position; having carefully reviewed all the materials sent by the university, they knew they'd have private disability insurance if it came to that. Or so they thought: after the accident they contacted the university, which in turn consulted its disability insurance provider. Only then was it revealed that the benefit included a one-year waiting period: my colleague was ineligible. As he puts it, that "rather salient fact" was not included in the university's written materials. Fortunately, he regained full mobility, but he and his wife were truly frightened by the incident. Universal public systems have fewer such cracks through which to fall.

The Central Importance of Deservingness

A second characteristic of the American welfare state is the strong influence of "deservingness" in the provision of protections from life's risks. While many social protections are conferred on a near-universal basis in other rich democracies, in the United States more generous benefits are given to groups deemed deserving, such as retired workers. Those perceived as less deserving, such as the non-working poor, are seemingly held responsible for their plights and given only meager help. As Lynch says, the welfare policies of western Europe and Canada reflect "the principle of inclusion with elements of universal entitlement based on need and adequacy," while the American welfare state instead "prioritizes personal responsibility, help for the deserving only, and the principle of less eligibility," thereby making public benefits less desirable than work, as we saw in chapter 4.

For the poor in America, the resulting orientation of the government is less about assistance than about skepticism, begrudging and meager help, concern about fraud, and even punishment.[41] These policies reflect public attitudes. As disability activist Dennis Heaphy says, "Americans have a punitive view of poverty and who is poor and why they are poor."[42] Many are very concerned that some people might get more than they deserve. Heaphy adds, "We live in a mindset of scarcity, and everyone is afraid that someone is getting away with something or taking away from them." In the policy regime that arises from these attitudes, social workers function as gatekeepers rather than facilitators, and scarce dollars are devoted to sorting the deserving from the undeserving. The inefficiency of these practices is demonstrated by the decision of many states to simply drop the Medicaid asset test rather than try to ferret out the tiny level of resources most Medicaid applicants have.

The Elderly Orientation of US Policy and Lack of Help for Working-Age Americans

A third notable feature of the American welfare state in cross-national comparison is its orientation toward the elderly.[43] Social Security and Medicare approximate the public pension and health insurance offerings of advanced-economy nations (although they have their own shortcomings, as we'll see below). But the United States spends much less on help for working-age adults and children, even when K–12 public education is included. The dearth of policies providing paid leave and child care for working parents and caregivers is one manifestation; the lack of effective job training programs and underinvestment in community colleges and public higher education is another. Protecting the elderly is an admirable goal, but the nonelderly need social protections as well, and economic growth requires robust investments in human capital, such as education and training. Thus, the American welfare state protects one part of the life course reasonably well, but leaves the others to the vagaries of the market.

The list of social protections for working-age people that are common in other countries but nonexistent in ours is long indeed. American employers aren't legally required to offer paid sick leave or paid vacation, as in many economically advanced nations. Incredibly, the United States is one of only four nations—out of 173 for which data are available—that doesn't offer paid maternity or parental leave for women (the other three are Liberia, Papua New Guinea, and Swaziland).[44] There is no national paid leave for family caregiving, either—just twelve weeks of unpaid leave for which only half are eligible and most can't afford to take.[45] Also unlike many other advanced-economy countries, there is no universal public day care or preschool: only 58 percent of American three- to five-year-olds attend preschool, compared with 90 to 100 percent in much of Europe.[46] Tax credits for child care don't come close to offsetting the full cost of day care, especially in metropolitan areas.[47] And despite the fact that federal TANF rules require mothers to work, with no exemptions for having to care for children or relatives (though states can have these), public child care programs for poor families are so underfunded that only a fraction of eligible children can actually enroll.[48] In other rich countries, housing assistance, lone-parent allowances, and family allowances are more generous than the analogous programs in the United States. There are also wage policies that make the gaps between full- and part-time pay smaller than in our country.[49]

In other words, families at all income levels are often on their own if they live in the United States. What's crazy about this system is that Americans work hard and yet get so little help to facilitate working. Consider the fact that nearly three-quarters of American mothers with children under the age of eighteen work, up from half in 1975.[50] In other words, in most households with children, all the adults work.

And they work long hours: 54 percent of dual-earner couples with children jointly work 80 to 99 hours per week, and another 10 percent work more than 100 hours. In the next-highest nation, Canada, those proportions were 34 percent and 5 percent, respectively. In Sweden, only 6 percent of couples work more than 80 hours per week.[51] Moreover, the American statistics aren't driven solely by hard-charging professionals working longer hours; over time, hours worked have increased in all income, education, and occupational groups.[52] And yet there are so few programs to help workers in the United States. There are no regulations on work hours as in other countries—how handy, given that many American families need to work long hours to make ends meet because of low wages. And there are very few supports for families, especially those with children or other caregiving obligations. Family members everywhere face "conflicts between earning and caring," but in the United States they are uniquely left to devise solutions themselves.[53] The lack of support is a huge issue—not just for the poor and those trying to exit social assistance, but also for the middle class, who often have difficulty covering these needs themselves.

Perhaps the success of paid family leave in California will pave the way for more universal social supports for working-age Americans. While federal policy grants twelve weeks of unpaid leave in case of personal illness, to care for a family member, or to care for a newborn or newly adopted child, few can afford to skip their paychecks. In the face of ineffective federal policy, California instituted a six-week paid leave in 2004; this is the leave that allowed Dave to stay with Marcella and Logan after the accident. A payroll tax on employees funds the program, which replaces 55 percent of wages up to a maximum weekly benefit of $987.[54]

Despite perennial arguments from the business sector that federal paid leave would add crippling costs, paid leave in California has been a "non-event," according to the main scholarly evaluation, with the vast majority of businesses surveyed saying that the program has had "no noticeable effect or a positive effect" on employee productivity, profitability, turnover, and morale. Smaller businesses report even more positive outcomes than larger employers. And for employees, paid leave has been a godsend. Surveyed workers at all wage levels who used the program were better able to care for their new child or ill family member, and more satisfied with the length of their leave. Going on paid leave doubled the number of weeks of breast-feeding for new mothers. And low-wage workers using paid leave were more likely to return to the same employer, reducing the costs of turnover.[55] Despite these state-level successes, there's virtually no movement toward a nationwide policy. Perhaps continued financial insecurity in the middle class will provide an impetus for change.

Limitations Even in the "Upper" Tier

As good as senior citizens have it in the American welfare state, even the upper-tier universal programs contain significant shortcomings.[56] Maybe it's not surprising to learn that cash assistance for the poor as a percentage of median household income is lower in the United States than elsewhere, even when food stamps are factored in. Or that the Child Tax Credit is worth less than family allowances in all other rich countries except Australia, New Zealand, and the United Kingdom. Or that there is far less vocational training. What is surprising is that even American upper-tier programs aren't as generous as in other countries. Even Social Security, the most vaunted and successful of our social programs, pays lower benefits as a percentage of preretirement wages than the public pension programs of other advanced-economy nations. And while many Americans without health insurance look at Medicare with envy, and can't wait until they become eligible at the age of 65, it imposes huge out-of-pocket costs and has many holes in its coverage. Fidelity Investments has calculated that a 65-year-old couple retiring in 2011 with an average life span (20 more years for the wife, 17 for the husband) would need $240,000 to cover their share of health care costs in retirement.[57] But only one in five people aged 55 to 64 has saved that much; nearly one-third have saved less than $10,000.[58] The American welfare state tilts heavily toward the elderly, and Social Security and Medicare are the most generous social programs we've got. Yet the poverty level among older Americans is the highest among rich nations.[59] Even our most expansive programs fall short of other nations' efforts.

Tremendous Geographic Variation in Social Policies

The fifth feature that sets American social policy apart is its vast geographic variation. In other countries, subnational governments similar in function to our states often administer social policy systems and even have fiscal responsibility for them, but virtually nowhere are they allowed to determine the content of policy and to deliver such wildly varying outcomes as in the United States. Nowhere else do social assistance payments differ by a 4-to-1 ratio from one part of the country to another, when the cost-of-living difference is only 1.4 to 1.[60] Nowhere else are covered personal care assistance hours allowed to vary from ten hours per day (North Dakota) to nothing (Tennessee until 2010). Nowhere else would 3 percent of the residents in one part of the country lack health insurance and 24 percent lack it in another part, as is the case with Massachusetts and Texas. No other advanced nation lets mere geography determine the nature of social protections or allows such disparate eligibility and benefit levels. In no other rich democracy does the nature of social citizenship vary so widely by location.

Misconceptions about Welfare States Elsewhere

American social policy lacks many crucial supports and leaves huge numbers of individuals and families without important protections. But many in this country are skeptical about the social policy systems of other rich nations. Misconceptions abound—that welfare states elsewhere are one size fits all, or that overly generous provisions undermine the incentives for work.[61] Two important points are worth noting.

First, most welfare states are like that of the United States in that they provide different levels of benefits to different levels of workers. Most welfare states stratify, conferring greater benefits to people who have higher earnings, work in higher-level jobs, or are otherwise "better employed." Where the United States clearly fails is in not providing a basic level of protection to everyone. This is most obvious, and most consequential, in the area of health care: while many of life's risks are foreseeable, and people might be expected to shoulder more of the resultant costs themselves (childbearing, old age), the need for health care is often unknowable, even sudden. That the United States does not guarantee health insurance for all citizens means that one unfortunate moment can upend an entire life, even for a hardworking person. And that's the difference: where every advanced-economy nation has inevitable gaps in its social protections, the United States has chasms.

Second, social protections in other countries are intended not to replace work but to support it. In market economies, whether in the United States or elsewhere, people work to support themselves and their families. But other rich democracies have far more programs in place to facilitate work, policies that help people balance their job with other obligations and needs, such as paid maternity and parental leave when they have a baby, subsidized child care when they have a young child, and paid sick days when they are ill. The purpose of social protections is not to create nonworkers but to help people work so that they can in turn pay taxes, earn entitlement to these protections, and financially support these and other government functions. In contrast, the United States has far fewer policies that facilitate work. That's peculiar, given that hard work is such a core American value and that working is so crucial because people must pay for so many needs out of pocket. What's contradictory is not a market economy combined with a social welfare state but rather a system that requires work but lacks the policies that make work possible.

Rich Nation, Poor Outcomes

We are accustomed to the United States being No. 1. Our nation has the largest economy in the world, and one of the highest gross domestic products per capita. Our culture of entrepreneurship and innovation continues to attract talented individuals from every corner of the globe. But the United States also has some terrible outcomes, partly due to the nature of our social policies. We're not No. 1 in everything. On a variety of health indicators, we rank at the bottom of the list of advanced industrialized nations because of less access to health care and greater poverty. In life expectancy at birth, we rank last for men and second to last for women among rich nations. We also rank worst for heart disease, lung disease, diabetes, and sexually transmitted diseases. Infant mortality rates are three times higher than in other rich countries.[62] Although Americans do have better access to high-tech diagnostic procedures such as MRIs, they are less able to get same- or next-day doctor appointments (per capita availability of doctors, doctor visits, and hospital beds is lower in the United States). They are less likely to have test results or medical records available at the time of their appointment. They are less likely to have chronic conditions such as diabetes or high blood pressure under control.[63] Outcomes in other areas are no better. American schoolchildren put in middling performances in international student assessments.[64] There is less intergenerational economic mobility in the United States than in other rich countries.[65] The nation does rank No. 1 in some undesirable categories: highest health care costs, highest preventable mortality, highest poverty rate, highest income inequality.[66]

Behind the statistics on the shortcomings of American social policy are real people. In any other rich democracy, Dave and Marcella wouldn't have had to become poor and stay poor for Marcella to have health insurance. In any other rich democracy, they could retain their savings and earnings and raise their son in the middle class. I would be able to help them financially without restriction. But not in the United States, where no matter your work ethic or industriousness or loving family, one bad moment can turn your whole life upside down.

THE FUTURE OF MEANS-TESTED PROGRAMS

The American system of social protections—and means-tested programs in particular—is stunningly inadequate, even cruel. And yet contemporary debates focus not on how to improve these programs but how to cut them. The contemporary manifestation of the less eligibility principle, the age-old skepticism toward the poor and needy, is to solve the nation's fiscal problems by reducing the size and scope of social programs, particularly social assistance.

Concern begins with the big social insurance programs, Social Security and Medicare—both their future cost and the long-term mismatch between the programs' promised benefits and projected revenues. Some reform proposals make tweaks within the programs' existing structures, such as changing the inflation adjustment for Social Security benefits, while others change the programs' structure by reducing the guaranteed benefits, either by partially privatizing Social Security or by turning Medicare into a voucher program.[67]

Many of the most Draconian reform proposals, however, center on cuts to social assistance programs. Many programs for the poor are part of domestic discretionary spending, which in budgetary reform proposals tends to get cut more deeply than defense or mandatory domestic spending.[68] The discretionary programs include food stamps, Head Start and child care programs, public housing and Section 8 housing vouchers, and heating assistance. And while Medicaid, along with Social Security and Medicare, is an entitlement program and therefore part of mandatory spending, a reform proposal that crops up perennially would turn the federal share of Medicaid into a block grant to the states. If the TANF block grant experience is any guide, this reform would have devastating effects, seriously eroding health insurance for the poor.

The appetite for cutting social assistance is demonstrated not just in these reform proposals but also in congressional votes—the forty-six votes in the House to repeal the ACA (as of October 1, 2013), the multiple votes to cut food stamps in 2012 and 2013—and in the design of the budget sequester that began on March 1, 2013. Sequestration originated in 2011, when congressional Republicans refused to raise the nation's debt ceiling unless President Obama agreed to deficit reduction. A supercommittee to create a deficit reduction package was set up, and a trigger put in place to incentivize a deal: a set of automatic spending cuts that would go into effect if a deal were not reached. The across-the-board cuts were intended to be so objectionable as to force action. Apparently, they weren't objectionable enough: the supercommittee failed to reach a deal, and the automatic spending cuts were made. These included cuts to Section 8 housing vouchers, long-term Unemployment Insurance benefits, and Head Start slots, among many other programs.

Behind the numbers, of course, are real people. Massachusetts gives out 20,000 Section 8 vouchers each year, but has 80,000 households on the waiting list. In Boston, a single mother named India Cox spent years on the Section 8 waiting list with her young daughter and was relieved to get a notice that a voucher was available. She had just begun looking for an apartment when a second letter arrived a few weeks later, rescinding the offer due to the sequestration budget cuts.[69] Similarly, more than 1,300 Head Start slots, and 120 jobs, were eliminated in Massachusetts for the 2013–14 school year. Another single mom, Laramii Wright, told the *Boston Globe* that she didn't know whether she could continue her job training if she couldn't find dependable child care for her son.[70]

For all the desire in some quarters to cut means-tested programs, or at least to stem their growth, the need for social assistance across the life span is likely to grow. The private welfare system of employer-provided benefits continues to shrink. The aged and disabled shares of the population are growing. Low and stagnant wages for low- and middle-income earners mean that people will be less able to meet the cost of health insurance or day care or unemployment spells or, later, to help cover their retirement or LTC needs. Smaller families mean fewer informal caregivers as well. The means-tested programs that have been allowed to grow are harbingers: Medicaid and CHIP covered almost 18 percent of the nonelderly population in 2011, up from 10 percent in 1999.[71] The number of Americans receiving food stamps more than doubled between 2000 and 2011, with much of that increase coming even before the Great Recession.[72] Rather than being a small, residual corner of the welfare state ripe for pruning, social assistance programs are increasingly important and, given larger economic and demographic forces on them, will become only more so.

Some say the government role in social assistance has grown too large, and that charitable organizations should make up the difference. Indeed, the United States has a long and honorable history of charity and philanthropy. In 2011, two-thirds of households gave to charity, accounting for three-quarters of all benevolent donations.[73] Such giving is certainly laudable, and goodness knows that Dave and Marcella have been the beneficiaries of some extraordinary efforts. But such generosity pales in comparison with public social program spending. Charitable giving in 2011 totaled $298 billion, which is wonderful, but that's what the federal government spent on Medicaid and CHIP alone that same year. Charity is a crucial supplement, but it can't be a substitute for government action.

Yet others assert that the United States can't do more in terms of social assistance because it would be too expensive and would drive up taxes, which are already too high. Of course, no one wants to pay higher taxes. And taxes that are too high can retard economic growth. But so can taxes that are too low, particularly when low revenues lead to insufficient investment in the future—in education and in programs that give poor children a leg up, for instance. It's worth noting that the United States has the lowest taxes among rich nations. Among the 34 nations in the Organisation for Economic Co-operation and Development, which includes both rich democracies and middle-income countries, it ranks third from the bottom in total taxes as a percentage of the economy (the two countries below the United States in 2011 were Turkey and Chile). Total taxes in the United States are just three-fourths those in France and Germany, half those in Denmark and Sweden.[74] Raising taxes by just a few percentage points of its gross domestic product would still leave the United States a very low-tax country and wouldn't harm its economic growth,[75] but *would* make a world of difference for needy Americans.

HARD TRUTHS AND CONTRADICTIONS
IN AMERICAN SOCIAL POLICY

Our family's experience with the American welfare state and the questions this experience led me to ask reveal several stark truths.

First, American social policy, both by design and in effect, has separate tiers for workers and nonworkers, and the lower, means-tested tier is large, not residual. Many observers would wish social assistance away, but in fact most Americans will encounter means-tested programs at some point in their lives. Economic and demographic changes are making them more important than ever.

Second, policy makers like to believe that means-tested programs are designed to give a hand up, but some are actually designed in a way that keeps people down. The need to stay poor to get benefits undercutting attempts to improve one's lot, the huge marginal tax rates as one leaves the programs—that's the price we have chosen to pay in our efforts to narrowly focus these programs on a tight subset of the truly needy. As currently designed, social assistance programs discourage work. They discourage marriage. They punish children for their parents' situation. Policy makers need to improve program design and to improve protections available from jobs and other social programs, to ease transitions out of social assistance. These programs should be a bridge to a more secure life, not a trap.

Third, Dave and Marcella's story shows that American citizens don't have equal access to economic security or health care, or even the same chance to save their own money and receive financial help from their families. It all depends on which state they live in. In recent years, we have heard a lot about extreme income and wealth inequality in the United States. But inequality based on geography can be just as pernicious, perhaps even more so, because it is dictated so overtly by government policy. Such differential treatment owing to the accident of location raises profound questions about the justice and morality of the social welfare system.

Fourth, it doesn't have to be this way. Other countries provide basic protections to all, regardless of a citizen's employment situation or location. They allow people to leave poverty with more training, better wages at the bottom end of the spectrum, and a more complete set of social benefits (health insurance, child care, and so on) that facilitate work. In the United States, people often can't help but be trapped in social assistance, because the health insurance and child care and other supports they need aren't sufficiently available from employers or other social programs. In providing wider protections, the United States wouldn't be contradicting American values of hard work and family—but too often, that's what happens now.

I worry that those who make social policy fail to comprehend what the requirements, rules, and regulations they create mean for the ordinary people who live under them. I hadn't fully—and studying social policy is my job. But until my family fell down the rabbit hole and experienced these things firsthand, I hadn't really understood or fully appreciated the ramifications of the design of the American welfare state.

In the end, pressure for change has to come from the American people. "We are all vulnerable," health policy expert Harold Pollack reminds us. "We have to take care of each other."[76] We *all* need help— if not today, then at some point in our lives. We have to protect each other against risks that would be crushing were we left to face them alone. I firmly hope and believe that we will be much more supportive of social protections for all when at last we internalize the reality that our lives could change in an instant—just as my family's has.

ACKNOWLEDGMENTS

My thanks go first and foremost to my brother and sister-in-law, Dave Campbell and Marcella Wagner, for allowing me to share their story and to illustrate how the American social policy system really works. It's one thing to read about these programs in dry, technocratic manuals meant for policy experts; it's quite another to see people you love living through them. Dave and Marcella have been remarkably generous with their time and willingness to shed some of their privacy so that others can see the reality of life in these means-tested programs. Their strength of character in the face of many profound challenges is humbling to witness.

I also thank our mother, Mary Ann Campbell, who dropped everything and moved eighteen hundred miles to help out with baby Logan. Our stepmother, Kathryn Kirkman Campbell, generously housed and fed the crew for months and months. The entire Wagner family helped with everything, from negotiating these programs for Marcella and Dave in the early months, to providing Marcella's personal care, to storing the couple's belongings while their house was under construction. I can't imagine what it would have been like for them without such strong family support.

We are enormously indebted to the dozens of nurses, doctors, social workers, and physical therapists who have helped the family in every imaginable way, from providing health care for my sister-in-law and nephew to assisting in navigating the mind-bogglingly complex world of welfare medicine and social assistance programs. The staffs of Mercy Medical Center and Santa Clara Valley Medical Center are extraordinary in their expertise, professionalism, thoughtfulness, and generosity.

Our family can never repay the debt we owe to the people of Redding, California, and surrounding communities for opening their hearts to Dave, Marcella, and Logan after the accident. We are truly grateful to the scores of friends and family members who worked so hard on Dave and Marcella's behalf. I choke up every time I think about the extraordinary love and commitment these incomparable individuals have shown. We cannot thank everyone here—doing so would add another chapter to the book—but we do want to give a special shout-out to Tim Sheehy, Bob Weir, Greg Wagner Jr., Neal Martin, Evan Johnson, Rob and Lisa Rose, Russ and Ruth Duclos, Dana and Jim Jordan, Leslie and Charles Kitzman, Rita Hosking, John and Sheri Dotter, John and Lisa Reed, Steve Ksenzulak, Jake and Ashley Fuller, Juli Heleniak, and Lisa Jeter of Jeterbuilt Construction. We are also grateful to the many other individuals and businesses who made donations to help renovate the house, as well as to the complete strangers from around the country who heard about Dave and Marcella's plight and reached out to help. I thank, too, my friends and professional colleagues who responded so generously when I came around rattling my tin cup.

In writing this book, I had very helpful conversations with Alan Cohen, Colleen Grogan, Jonathan Lazar, Ruth Milkman, Kimberly Morgan, Mark Peterson, Harold Pollack, Kathy Swartz, Joshua Wiener, and Anthony Wright. Interviews with Deborah Cunningham, Tony Dreyfus, Dennis Heaphy, Lisa Iezzoni, and Michael Ogg helped me understand many aspects of policy and people's experiences on the ground. I am thankful to Blair Read, who assisted with research, editorial suggestions, proofreading, and manuscript preparation with her trademark alacrity. I also thank the state-level Medi-Cal officials who graciously helped me try to sort out Dave and Marcella's status. They needed to remain anonymous but were very helpful. If I sound frustrated in these pages, I hope they realize that I know that the fault lies with the program and its astonishing complexity, not with them. I am very grateful for their assistance.

A number of generous individuals read chapters and in some cases the entire manuscript, and I so appreciate their time and their insights: Deborah Bachrach, Kathryn Kirkman Campbell, Allen Feinstein, Hahrie Han, Andy Karch, Frank Levy, Julie Lynch, Lisa Miller, Kimberly Morgan, Harold Pollack, Joe Soss, Frank Thompson, Craig

Volden, and Dave and Marcella. The reviewers for the University of Chicago Press provided invaluable comments. Deborah Stone, who revealed her identity from the outset, gave me the most thorough, insightful, provocative, and constructive comments I have ever seen on a manuscript. This book has meant more to me than anything I have ever written, and Deborah seemed as invested in the project as I was. I am truly touched by her commitment to helping me improve it in so many ways.

A previously scheduled but fortuitously timed sabbatical from MIT and a fellowship at the Radcliffe Institute for Advanced Study gave me the time to write this book alongside my official project for the leave year. Many thanks to Judy Vichniac, Sharon Bromberg-Lin, Rebecca Haley, Liz Cohen, and my fellow fellows. I also thank Patty Tang and Nathan Cisneros, who pinch-hit for me at MIT after the accident, and then-department head Rick Locke and the departmental staff and faculty for being so supportive during a difficult period.

I am grateful to Aaron Retica of the *New York Times* who helped me bring Dave and Marcella's story to life with editorial incisiveness and great compassion. The book wouldn't exist if not for series editor Larry Jacobs, who urged me to write it in the first place and who was an incredible cheerleader and champion all along. John Tryneski of the University of Chicago Press has been unimaginably supportive and committed to the project, and a font of good ideas and advice to boot. Many thanks to Rodney Powell, Sandra Hazel, Melinda Kennedy, and the many others at the press who worked so hard on behalf of this project.

NOTES

CHAPTER ONE

1 US Census Bureau, 2012 Statistical Abstract, "Personal Income per Capita in Current and Constant Dollars by State" (Washington, DC: US Department of Commerce, 2012), table 681.

2 This figure is the median household income in 2011. Carmen DeNavas-Walt, Bernadette D. Proctor, and Jessica C. Smith, "Income, Poverty and Health Insurance Coverage in the United States: 2011," US Census Bureau, Current Population Reports, P60-243 (Washington, DC: Government Printing Office, September 2012), 5.

3 The Economic Policy Institute's Family Budget Calculator "measures the income a family needs in order to attain a secure yet modest living standard by estimating community-specific costs of housing, food, child care, transportation, health care, other necessities, and taxes" for 615 US communities in 2013. The $60,482 figure is for a two-adult, one-child family in the Redding, California, metropolitan statistical area. See Economic Policy Institute, "Family Budget Calculator," accessed February 28, 2014, http://www.epi.org/resources/budget/.

4 US and California unemployment rates for February 2012 from the US Department of Labor, Bureau of Labor Statistics, "Regional and State Employment and Unemployment—February 2012," http://www.bls.gov/news.release/archives/laus_03302012.pdf. The Shasta County unemployment rate is for the July 2011–August 2012 period, from the US Department of Labor, Bureau of Labor Statistics, "Local Area Unemployment Statistics," accessed February 28, 2014, http://www.bls.gov/lau/laucntycur14.txt.

5 UCLA Center for Health Policy Research, 2009 California Health Interview Survey, http://ask.chis.ucla.edu/main/DQ3/geographic.asp.

6 US Census Bureau, "Poverty: 2010 and 2011," September 2012, http://www.census.gov/prod/2012pubs/acsbr11-01.pdf.

7 US Department of Labor, Bureau of Labor Statistics, "The 30 Occupations with the Largest Projected Employment Growth, 2010–2020," accessed February 28, 2014, http://www.bls.gov/news.release/ecopro.t06.htm.

8 American Association of Colleges of Nursing, "Nursing Shortage Fact Sheet," August 6, 2012, http://www.aacn.nche.edu/media-relations/NrsgShortageFS.pdf.

9 A 2009 National Women's Law Center study found that only 13 percent of individual market policies provide maternity coverage. The 1978 Pregnancy Discrimination Act requires maternity coverage, but not for firms that have fewer than fifteen employees or individual insurance policies. See Michelle Andrews, "Many Individual Health Policies Do Not Cover Pregnancy," *Kaiser Health News*, November 16, 2010, http://www.kaiserhealthnews.org/features/insuring-your-health/maternity-expenses.aspx. On the experience of a professional couple whose health insurance does not cover maternity care, see Elisabeth Rosenthal, "American Way of Birth, Costliest in the World," *New York Times*, June 30, 2013. Precisely because of these shortcomings, the Affordable Care Act of 2010 requires insurance plans offered in the individual and small-group markets (the health insurance exchanges) to cover maternity and newborn care. US Department of Health and Human Services, ASPE Issue Brief, "Essential Health Benefits: Individual Market Coverage," December 16, 2011, http://aspe.hhs.gov/health/reports/2011/IndividualMarket/ib.shtml.

10 State of California, "AIM Income Guidelines," April 1, 2013, http://www.aim.ca.gov/Costs/Income_Guidelines.aspx. For the income eligibility calculation, the pregnant woman counts as two persons. On AIM's budgetary limit, the program website states, "The number of women enrolling in AIM is limited by state funding. While adequate funding is generally available, once the program is full, you will not be enrolled even if you qualify and your application is complete. If this happens, you will be notified by mail, and your initial payment will be refunded." See State of California, "Who Can Qualify?," accessed February 28, 2014, http://www.aim.ca.gov/AIM_Program/.

11 Thanks to Deborah Stone for these characterizations.

12 This 15 percent figure reflects the traditional definition of the federal poverty line, which was created in 1963 by Social Security Administration research analyst Mollie Orshansky. She tallied the cost of the "economy food plan," the cheapest of the USDA's four food plans, and multiplied by 3. Since then, the figures have been adjusted for inflation (see US Social Security Administration, "Remembering Mollie Orshansky—The Developer of the Poverty Thresholds," accessed February 28, 2014, http://www.ssa.gov/policy/docs/ssb/v68n3/v68n3p79.html). Many observers believe that the official poverty line is too low. For example, the Economic Policy Institute's Family Budget Calculator found that across 615 cities, it takes an income of more than twice the federal poverty line for a family to afford basic expenses. See Economic Policy Institute, "Family Budget Calculator." International comparisons typically measure poverty as some percentage of a nation's median wage.

13 Danilo Trisi, Arkic Sherman, and Matt Broaddus, "Poverty Rate Second-Highest in 45 Years; Record Numbers Lacked Health Insurance, Lived in Deep Poverty," Center on Budget and Policy Priorities, September 14, 2011, 8; http://www.cbpp.org/cms/?fa=view&id=3580.

14 Timothy M. Smeeding, Lee Rainwater, and Gary Burtless, "U.S. Poverty in a Cross-National Context," in *Understanding Poverty*, ed. Sheldon Danziger and Robert Haveman (New York: Russell Sage Foundation, 2001), 181.

15 Catherine Rampell, "Majority of Jobs Added in the Recovery Pay Low Wages, Study Finds," *New York Times*, August 31, 2012.

16 This statistic and the remainder in this paragraph are from Steven Greenhouse, "Productivity Climbs, but Wages Stagnate," *New York Times Sunday Review*, January 13, 2013.

17 Anthony B. Atkinson, Thomas Piketty, and Emmanuel Saez, "Top Incomes in the Long Run of History," *Journal of Economic Literature* 49, no. 1 (2011): 3–71; the 65% figure cited in the text is from p. 9.

18 Floyd Norris, "U.S. Companies Thrive as Workers Fall Behind," *New York Times*, August 10, 2013.

19 In 2010, the median full-time male worker with a bachelor's degree earned $64,000, compared with $40,000 for a high school graduate. See National Center for Education Statistics, "Median Annual Earnings of Year-Round Full-Time Workers 25 and Over, by Highest Level of Educational Attainment and Sex: 1990 through 2010," accessed February 28, 2014, http://nces.ed.gov/programs/digest/d11/tables/dt11_395.asp.

20 Lawrence Mishel, Josh Bivens, Elise Gould, and Heidi Shierholz, eds., "College Wage Premium by Gender," in *The State of Working America*, 12th ed. (Ithaca, NY: Cornell University Press, 2012), accessed February 28, 2014, http://stateofworkingamerica.org/chart/swa-wages-figure-4n-college-wage-premium/.

21 Thomas G. Mortenson, "Family Income and Unequal Educational Opportunity, 1970–2011," *Postsecondary Education Opportunity* 245 (November 2012).

22 Urban Institute, "Five Questions on Workforce Development Policy," May 26, 2011, http://www.urban.org/toolkit/fivequestions/Nightingale-Workforce-Development.cfm.

23 David H. Autor and David Dorn, "The Growth of Low Skill Service Jobs and the Polarization of the U.S. Labor Market," *American Economic Review* 103, no. 5 (August 2013): 1553–97.

24 DeNavas-Walt, Proctor, and Smith, "Income, Poverty and Health Insurance Coverage in the United States: 2011," 21. Many people have multiple sources of health insurance (for example, a Medicare beneficiary who also has a di-

rectly purchased "medigap" supplemental policy, or a veteran who has some military care through the Department of Veterans Affairs but also employer-provided insurance. In 2011, Americans had the following types of health insurance (the first number is the percentage having that form of insurance; the second number is the percentage having that form of insurance alone): any private plan (63.9/52.0); employment-based (55.1/45.1); direct-purchase (9.8/3.6); any government plan (32.2/20.4); Medicare (15.2/4.9); Medicaid (16.5/11.5); and military health care (4.4/1.3); see ibid., 25.

25 Ibid., 21.

26 Paul Fronstin, "Employment-Based Health Benefits: Trends in Access and Coverage, 1997–2010," Employee Benefit Research Institute Issue Brief no. 370, April 2012, http://www.ebri.org/pdf/briefspdf/EBRI_IB_04-2012_N0370_HI-Trends.pdf. Not surprisingly, uninsurance rates are particularly high among those whose employer does not sponsor health benefits: 50 percent in 2010 (the other half were able to get insurance through a spouse, public coverage, or individually purchased policies).

27 Paul Fronstin, "Sources of Health Insurance and Characteristics of the Uninsured: Analysis of the March 2012 Current Population Survey," Employee Benefit Research Institute Issue Brief no. 376, September 2012, 14, http://www.ebri.org/publications/ib/index.cfm?fa=ibDisp&content_id=5114. Those working in small firms often get insurance through a spouse, which was Dave and Marcella's plan for the future, or from a public program.

28 DeNavas-Walt, Proctor, and Smith, "Income, Poverty and Health Insurance Coverage in the United States: 2011," 22.

29 Ibid., 25.

30 Fronstin, "Employment-Based Health Benefits," 19.

31 Cathy Schoen, Sara R. Collins, Jennifer L. Kriss, and Michelle M. Doty, "How Many Are Underinsured? Trends among U.S. Adults, 2003 and 2007," Health Affairs 27 (July 2008): W298–W309.

32 Health Access, "Protecting Consumers from Medical Debt," August 2009, www.health-access.org.

33 David U. Himmelstein, Elizabeth Warren, Deborah Thorne, and Steffie Woolhandler, "Illness and Injury as Contributors to Bankruptcy," Health Affairs 24 (February 2005): W5–W63.

34 See the debate between Himmelstein (ibid.) and David Dranove and Michael L. Millenson, "Medical Bankruptcy: Myth versus Fact," Health Affairs 25, no. 2 (2006): W74–W83.

35 The main finding of the Oregon Health Insurance Experiment Project, in which the state expanded its Medicaid program by lottery in 2008, allowing

researchers to study the effects of randomly assigned health insurance, is that having insurance did not change the prevalence or diagnosis of high blood pressure or high cholesterol, but it did significantly increase diabetes detection and management, reduce rates of depression, increase use of preventive services, and almost eliminate catastrophically high out-of-pocket medical expenditures. Thus, one conclusion is that health insurance fosters financial security. See Katherine Baicker et al., "The Oregon Experiment—Effects of Medicaid on Clinical Outcomes," *New England Journal of Medicine* 368, no. 18 (May 2, 2013): 1713–22.

36 Steven Greenhouse, "On Register's Other Side, Little Money to Spend," *New York Times*, November 29, 2013.

37 Economic Policy Institute, "Family Budget Calculator."

38 Stephen Brobeck, "Understanding the Emergency Savings Needs of Low- and Moderate-Income Households: A Survey-Based Analysis of Impacts, Causes, and Remedies," Consumer Federation of America, November 2008, http://www.csrees.usda.gov/nea/economics/pdfs/understandingTheEmergencySavingsNeedsOfLow_102908.pdf.

39 US Department of Labor, "Women in the Labor Force: A Databook," December 2011, table 7, http://www.bls.gov/cps/wlf-databook2011.htm.

40 Elizabeth Warren and Amelia Warren Tyagi, *The Two-Income Trap: Why Middle-Class Mothers and Fathers Are Going Broke* (New York: Basic Books, 2003), 65.

41 Ibid., 51. On increasing financial risks due to changes in the labor market and public policy, see Jacob S. Hacker, *The Great Risk Shift* (New York: Oxford University Press, 2006).

CHAPTER TWO

1 Specifically, states must extend Medicaid coverage to pregnant women and children under the age of six whose family incomes fall below 133 percent of the federal poverty line; children between six and years, below 100 percent of the FPL; and most SSI recipients. Kaiser Commission on the Medicaid and the Uninsured, "Medicaid: An Overview of Spending on 'Mandatory' vs. 'Optional' Populations and Services," June 2005, http://www.kff.org/medicaid/upload/Medicaid-An-Overview-of-Spending-on.pdf; Center on Budget and Policy Priorities, "Policy Basics: Introduction to Medicaid," December 17, 2008, http://www.cbpp.org/cms/index.cfm?fa=view&id=2223.

2 There are multiple ways to be eligible for Medi-Cal. Marcella is eligible because she qualified for a Supplemental Security Income benefit. She qualified for an SSI benefit because she (1) meets Social Security's definition of

disability; (2) is not doing "substantial gainful activity," meaning that her gross earnings are less than $1,010 per month in 2012; (3) has less than $3,000 in assets (for a couple; $3,150 because they have a child); and (4) has Total Countable Income that is less than the SSI maximum benefit amount (currently $1,444.20 for a couple living independently). The Total Countable Income calculation is complex. Total Countable Income = Countable Unearned Income plus Countable Earned Income. Countable Unearned Income = Monthly Unearned Income (as from SSI, Social Security Disability Insurance, a pension, interest, dividends, Short-Term Disability Insurance, or Long-Term Disability Insurance) minus a $20 General Income Exclusion. Countable Earned Income = Monthly Earned Income (as from a job) minus $65 Earned Income Exclusion minus half the remaining earned income minus $20 General Income Exclusion (if didn't already apply it to unearned income) minus Impairment Related Work Expenses, if any. Because Marcella is married, she is subject to "deeming": spouse's income and assets are added to those of the disabled person in all the above. Complicated enough? The Social Security Administration performs this calculation for SSI eligibility, and then reports one's Medi-Cal eligibility (which is automatic, if one qualifies for SSI) to the local county welfare office. See World Institute on Disability, Disability Benefits 101, "Medi-Cal: The Details; SSI-Linked Medi-Cal," accessed February 28, 2014, http://ca.db101.org/ca/programs/health_coverage/medi_cal/program2A.htm.

3 Later, a state Medi-Cal official told me that if I paid for preschool directly, this would not interfere with Marcella's Medi-Cal eligibility—that in calculating a recipient's income, the state imputes income provided in-kind for food, shelter, and clothing. Thus, if I provided any of those items, I would threaten her eligibility, but not if I paid for items beyond those three categories, including day care. That I can pay for day care but not for groceries is the opposite of what we learned from the hospital social worker. I don't know who to believe.

4 They are allowed to keep their furniture, wedding rings, clothing, cell phones, computers, and other exempt items. It is generally financial assets and vehicles that have to be liquidated.

5 Rourke O'Brien, "529s and Public Assistance: Asset Limits as a Barrier to College Savings," New American Foundation, November 2009, http://newamerica.net/publications/policy/529s_and_public_assistance. Medi-Cal recipients can save for college in Coverdell Educational Savings Accounts, although the maximum annual cap is just $2,000 (and had been only $500

until the American Taxpayer Relief Act of 2012 increased it). The child of a Medi-Cal recipient could have a Uniform Transfer to Minors Account under his or her Social Security number as long as the custodian is someone other than the parents; the child then has access to that money at the age of eighteen. However, UTMA accounts are taxable, and the tax bill goes to the parents. Thus, the college savings vehicles allowed by Medi-Cal are less attractive than 529 accounts—Coverdell ESAs because the limit is low, UTMA accounts because they are taxable.

6   State of California Department of Health Care Services, "Medi-Cal Estate Recovery Program," accessed February 28, 2014, http://www.dhcs.ca.gov/ formsandpubs/documents/dhcs9059_er_broch_en.pdf; and California Advocates for Nursing Home Reform, "Medi-Cal Recovery Frequently Asked Questions," July 24, 2013, http://www.canhr.org/factsheets/medi-cal_fs/html/ fs_medcal_recovery_FAQ.htm. If Logan were disabled, the state would not begin estate recovery until after his death.

7   For example, a 2011 study of Illinois medical specialty clinics found that 66 percent of children with Medicaid or Children's Health Insurance Program coverage were denied an appointment for specialist care, compared with just 11 percent of privately insured children. The Medicaid/CHIP children who were granted appointments had to wait twenty-one days longer than children with private insurance. Joanna Bisgaier and Karin V. Rhodes, "Access to Specialty Care for Children with Public Insurance," *New England Journal of Medicine* 364 (June 16, 2011): 2324–33.

8   For historical reasons outlined in chapter 5, note 74.

9   Note that in a money-saving move, the 2012–13 California state budget eliminated Healthy Families, requiring enrolled children to transition to Medi-Cal effective January 1, 2013. The benefits in the two programs are nearly identical, but the provider reimbursement levels are lower and provider networks narrower in Medi-Cal, raising concerns that some families will have difficulty locating physicians who will see their children. See Shelley Kessler and Anne Wilson, "Children's Health: California's Shift from Healthy Families to Medi-Cal May Harm Kids," *San Jose Mercury News*, March 4, 2013.

10 Many thanks to Lisa Iezzoni for these definitions. The Centers for Medicare and Medicaid Services, the federal agency that runs Medicaid, describes community-based long-term services and supports in this way: "CMS is working in partnership with states, consumers and advocates, providers and other stakeholders to create a sustainable, person-driven long-term support system in which people with disabilities and chronic conditions have choice, control

and access to a full array of quality services that assure optimal outcomes, such as independence, health and quality of life." US Department of Health and Human Services, Centers for Medicare and Medicaid Services, Medicaid .gov, "Long-Term Services and Supports," accessed February 28, 2014, http://www.medicaid.gov/Medicaid-CHIP-Program-Information/By-Topics/Long-Term-Services-and-Support/Long-Term-Services-and-Support.html.

11 Institute of Medicine, *The Future of Disability in America* (Washington, DC: National Academies Press, 2007), 268–73.

12 California Department of Social Services, "In Home Support Services (IHSS) Program," accessed February 28, 2014, http://www.cdss.ca.gov/agedblind disabled/pg1296.htm.

13 California Association of Public Authorities for IHSS, "CAPA Survey on IHSS Wages as of May 28, 2012," May 29, 2012, http://www.capaihss.org/_2009/home/faqs/wg_bn_052812.pdf.

14 Institute of Medicine, *The Future of Disability*.

15 California Foundation for Independent Living Centers, "What Is an Independent Living Center," accessed February 28, 2014, http://www.cfilc.org/site/c.fnJFKLNnFmG/b.5192463/k.5B10/What_is_an_Independent_Living _Center.htm.

16 Specifically, such states obtained waivers from the federal government that allow them to use Medicaid dollars for these home-based items. Institute of Medicine, *The Future of Disability*, 263–64.

17 Specifically, the café owner gave Marcella's brother-in-law the money, which went toward the house renovation. Dave and Marcella never had the money in hand.

18 World Institute on Disability, Disability Benefits 101, "Medi-Cal: The Basics," January 10, 2014, http://ca.db101.org/ca/programs/health_coverage/medi _cal/program.htm.

19 The share of cost for ABD-Medically Needy Medi-Cal can be enormous: it is the difference between a family's "countable income" (usually half their monthly earned income minus a deduction of $85 and any health plan premiums—for example, if they pay for a dental plan) and the amount of money they are allowed to retain to live on, the "family maintenance need level," which was last changed in 1989. The current MNL for a family of three is only $934. See Consumer Health Alliance, "ABD-Medically Needy Medi-Cal for Persons Who Are Aged, Blind, or have Disabilities," October 2007, http://healthconsumer.org/cs044ABD-MN.pdf.

20 Andrea Louise Campbell, "Down the Insurance Rabbit Hole," *New York Times*, April 5, 2012.

CHAPTER THREE

1 Michael Katz, *The Price of Citizenship: Redefining the American Welfare State* (New York: Henry Holt, 2001), 9.

2 Mark R. Rank and Thomas A. Hirschl, "Welfare Use as a Life Course Event: Toward a New Understanding of the U.S. Safety Net," *Social Work* 47 (July 2002): 237–48. See also Matt Breunig, "The High Probability of Being Poor," *American Prospect*, August 20, 2013, http://prospect.org/article/high-probability -being-poor.

3 US Department of Agriculture, Supplemental Nutrition Assistance Program monthly data, accessed February 28, 2014, http://www.fns.usda.gov/ pd/34snapmonthly.htm; US Department of Health and Human Services, Centers for Medicare and Medicaid Services, accessed February 28, 2014, Medicaid.gov, http://www.medicaid.gov/Medicaid-CHIP-Program-Information/ By-Population/Pregnant-Women/Pregnant-Women.html.

4 Author calculations using the Consumer Price Index. Note also that as of January 1, 2012, 18 states plus the District of Columbia have minimum wages higher than the federal level (the highest was $9.04 in Washington State), while 23 states' minimum wages equal the federal, 4 have lower than the federal-level wage, and 5 do not have a minimum wage requirement. Where state and federal minimum wages differ, the higher standard applies. US Department of Labor, Wages and Hour Division, "Minimum Wage Laws in the States—January 1, 2012," http://www.dol.gov/whd/minwage/america. htm#Consolidated. In 2014, President Obama proposed raising the federal minimum wage to $10.10, but congressional Republicans opposed the change.

5 Economic Policy Institute, "Share of Workers Earning Poverty-Level Wages, by Gender, 1973–2011," updated May 14, 2012, accessed March 4, 2014, http:// stateofworkingamerica.org/chart/swa-wages-figure-4e-share-workers -earning/.

6 Congressional Budget Office, "Trends in Earnings Variability over the Past 20 Years," April 2007, 7, https://www.cbo.gov/sites/default/files/cbofiles/ ftpdocs/80xx/doc8007/04-17-earningsvariability.pdf. Likewise, earnings can rise: 29 percent of workers experience a 25 percent increase in earnings, while 24 percent experience a 50 percent increase.

7 See Austin Nichols and Melissa M. Favreault, "The Impact of Changing Earnings Volatility on Retirement Wealth," Center for Retirement Research, Boston College, Working Paper 2008–14 (October 2008), for a review of the literature. The CBO says volatility has not increased, but most other researchers have found that it has. In their own analysis, Nichols and Favreault find that

individuals' income volatility has been flat over the last several decades, but that the volatility of family income has increased considerably.

8 Tim Casey and Laurie Maldonado, "Worst Off—Single-Parent Families in the United States: A Cross-National Comparison of Single Parenthood in the U.S. and Sixteen Other High-Income Countries," Women's Legal Defense and Education Fund, December 2012, http://www.legalmomentum.org/sites/default/files/reports/worst-off-single-parent.pdf.

9 Organisation for Economic Co-operation and Development, OECD iLibrary, OECD Employment and Labour Market Statistics, "Minimum Wages Relative to Median Wages," accessed February 28, 2014, http://www.oecd-ilibrary.org.libproxy.mit.edu/employment/data/earnings/minimum-wages-relative-to-median-wages_data-00313-en.

10 Many of these means-tested programs were established during president Franklin Roosevelt's New Deal of the 1930s (welfare, cash aid to the poor elderly and blind, and public housing) and president Lyndon Johnson's Great Society of the 1960s (Medicaid and food stamps, although precursors of the latter date back to 1939). Although popular perception is that these two liberal bursts of legislation produced the most programs for the poor, in fact many were established outside those eras: the school lunch program in 1946; Social Security Disability Insurance in 1956; SSI, which nationalized cash assistance for the poor elderly, disabled, and blind, in 1972; Section 8 housing vouchers in 1974; and the Children's Health Insurance Program in 1997, after the collapse of the Clinton administration's health reform effort. See Christopher Howard, *The Welfare State Nobody Knows: Debunking Myths about U.S. Social Policy* (Princeton, NJ: Princeton University Press, 2007), 60–61.

11 One example of how complex application procedures are: in 2010, the number of questions on a state Medicaid application ranged from 49 in New Mexico to 248 in Michigan; one-fourth of the states required an in-person interview or frequent recertification. See Donald P. Moynihan, Pamela Herd, and Elizabeth Rigby, "Policymaking by Other Means: Do States Use Administrative Barriers to Limit Access to Medicaid?," *Administration & Society*, published online September 19, 2013, http://www.lafollette.wisc.edu/facultystaff/moynihan/moynihan-herd-rigby-06-13-13.pdf.

12 US Department of Health and Human Services Poverty Guidelines at http://aspe.hhs.gov/poverty/12poverty.shtml, accessed February 28, 2014.

13 Kaiser Family Foundation, "Performing under Pressure: Annual Findings of a 50-State Survey of Eligibility, Enrollment, Renewal, and Cost-Sharing Politics in Medicaid and CHIP, 2011–12," January 2012, http://www.kff.org/medicaid/upload/8272.pdf.

14 Lynn M. Olson, Suk-fong S. Tang, and Paul W. Newacheck, "Children in the United States with Discontinuous Health Insurance Coverage," *New England Journal of Medicine* 353 (July 28, 2005): 382–91.

15 Stan Dorn and Genevieve M. Kenney, "Automatically Enrolling Eligible Children and Families into Medicaid and SCHIP: Opportunities, Obstacles, and Options for Federal Policymakers," Commonwealth Fund, June 2006, accessed March 5, 2014, http://www.commonwealthfund.org/Publications/ Fund-Reports/2006/Jun/Automatically-Enrolling-Eligible-Children-and -Families-Into-Medicaid-and-SCHIP—Opportunities—Obsta.aspx.

16 Fay Lomax Cook and Edith J. Barrett, *Support for the American Welfare State: The Views of Congress and the Public* (New York: Columbia University Press, 1992); Martin Gilens, *Why Americans Hate Welfare: Race, Media and the Politics of Antipoverty Policy* (Chicago: University of Chicago Press, 1999).

17 A proportion of a state's caseload can be exempted from the five-year limit, and states can spend their own money on recipients who exceed the five-year limit on federal aid. Postreform, less than 30 percent of TANF funds go toward cash assistance; the rest goes to encouraging employment and funding healthy marriage and responsible fatherhood initiatives. See US House Ways and Means Committee, *2012 Greenbook*, chapter 7: "Temporary Assistance for Needy Families," introduction, http://greenbook.waysandmeans.house .gov/2012-green-book. On welfare reform, see R. Kent Weaver, *Ending Welfare as We Know It* (Washington, DC: Brookings Institution Press, 2000); Charles Noble, *Welfare as We Knew It: A Political History of the American Welfare State* (New York: Oxford University Press, 1997); and Joe Soss, Richard C. Fording, and Sanford F. Schram, *Disciplining the Poor: Neoliberal Paternalism and the Persistent Power of Race* (Chicago: University of Chicago Press, 2011).

18 Originally, AFDC was an entitlement program, at least for the states, which received a share of federal funding for as many recipients as they deemed eligible. In practice, it was never an entitlement program for individuals in the way that Social Security and Medicare are; local discretion meant that many poor mothers were never deemed eligible in the first place, or had their benefits taken away through "morals tests" and other means, for which recipients had almost no procedural recourse. Welfare rights victories in the courts during the 1960s improved the situation for recipients somewhat. However, under TANF, federal funding is capped: the block grant for each state is set at the federal government's peak expenditure between FY1992 and FY1995 on cash welfare, emergency aid, and job training programs for welfare families. Gene Falk, "The Temporary Assistance for Needy Families (TANF) Block Grant: A Primer on TANF Financing and Federal Requirements," Congres-

sional Research Service, October 12, 2011, accessed March 5, 2014, http://
greenbook.waysandmeans.house.gov/sites/greenbook.waysandmeans
.house.gov/files/2011/images/RL32748%20v2_gb.pdf, p. 3. On growing antipathy toward welfare and the increasingly racialized image of the program
as motivations for reform, see Gilens, *Why Americans Hate Welfare*; and Soss,
Fording, and Schram, *Disciplining the Poor*.

19 Congressional Budget Office, "Growth in Means-Tested Programs and Tax
Credits for Low-Income Households," February 2013, http://www.cbo.gov/
sites/default/files/cbofiles/attachments/43934-Means-TestedPrograms.pdf.

20 US House Ways and Means Committee, *2011 Greenbook*, table 7–9.

21 Some people believe that food stamps or SSI has made up the difference.
They have not. Thanks to Harold Pollack for this point.

22 Edward G. Goetz, *New Deal Ruins: Race, Economic Justice, and Public Housing
Policy* (Ithaca, NY: Cornell University Press, 2013).

23 Center on Budget and Policy Priorities, "Federal Rental Assistance," January 25, 2013, http://www.cbpp.org/cms/?fa=view&id=3890. In both the public
housing and the rent subsidy programs, the tenant pays 30 percent of his
or her income in rent, with a minimum of $25 to $50. See J. A. Stoloff, "A
Brief History of Public Housing," US Department of Housing and Urban Development, Office of Policy Development and Research (no date), accessed
February 28, 2014, http://reengageinc.org/research/brief_history_public
_housing.pdf; Center on Budget and Policy Priorities, "Introduction to Pub-
lic Housing," January 25, 2013, accessed March 5, 2014, http://www.cbpp.org/
cms/?fa=view&id=2528m; and Center on Budget and Policy Priorities, "Federal Rental Assistance," January 25, 2013, accessed March 5, 2014, http://www
.cbpp.org/cms/index.cfm?fa=view&id=3890. While public housing originally
included middle-income people, seen as a stabilizing force, rule changes
and constrained funding over time made such housing less attractive to
higher-income residents, who moved out. Currently, households must have
income below 80 percent of the local median income, although eligibility
is set at 50 percent of the local median in some locales; about 70 percent of
those receiving rental assistance are below the poverty level.

24 Lawrence D. Brown and Michael S. Sparer, "Poor Program's Progress: The
Unanticipated Politics of Medicaid Policy," *Health Affairs* 22, no. 1 (January
2003): 31–44; Shanna Rose, *Financing Medicaid: Federalism and the Growth of
America's Health Care Safety Net* (Ann Arbor: University of Michigan Press,
2013).

25 Howard, *The Welfare State Nobody Knows*, 102–5.

26 US Department of Health and Human Services, Centers for Medicare and Medicaid Services, "2012 Actuarial Report on the Financial Outlook for Medicaid," http://medicaid.gov/Medicaid-CHIP-Program-Information/By-Topics/Financing-and-Reimbursement/Downloads/medicaid-actuarial-report-2012 .pdf, pp. iii, 22.

27 Congressional Budget Office, "Growth in Means-Tested Programs and Tax Credits for Low-Income Households," February 2013, 17.

28 Deirdre Walsh, "U.S. House Approves Farm Bill without Food Stamp Aid," CNN, July 12, 2013, http://www.cnn.com/2013/07/11/politics/house-farm-bill.

29 Congressional Budget Office, "Growth in Means-Tested Programs and Tax Credits for Low-Income Households," February 2013, 14.

30 US Social Security Administration, Annual Statistical Supplement, 2012, "Supplemental Security Income," table 7.A1, http://www.ssa.gov/policy/docs/statcomps/supplement/2012/7a.html.

31 Thanks to Harold Pollack for this observation.

32 US Social Security Administration, Annual Statistical Supplement, 2012, table 5.D1, http://www.ssa.gov/policy/docs/statcomps/supplement/2012/5d .html. SSDI payments are pegged to one's wages as a worker, so this is an average figure across all SSDI recipients.

33 Center on Budget and Policy Priorities, "Policy Basics: Introduction to the Supplemental Nutrition Assistance Program (SNAP)," March 28, 2013, http://www.cbpp.org/cms/index.cfm?fa=view&id=2226.

34 In 2011, the US Census Bureau and the Bureau of Labor Statistics introduced a new Supplemental Poverty Measure that included not just the value of cash transfers but also the value of in-kind benefits such as food stamps, housing assistance, and the school lunch program. The measure also includes the value of tax credits and makes other adjustments, such as accounting for geographic variation in housing costs. The idea was to account for the value of supports beyond cash assistance in determining whether someone was "poor." It turns out that including these adjustments made overall poverty worse: 16 percent under the Supplemental Poverty Measure, compared with 15.2 percent under the official poverty measure in 2010. See Lawrence Mishel, Josh Bivens, Elise Gould, and Heidi Shierholz, eds., *The State of Working America*, 12th ed. (Ithaca, NY: Cornell University Press, 2012), 430. Note that compared with the official poverty line, the Supplemental Poverty Measure reports less poverty among children and more poverty among the elderly.

35 Alfred Stepan and Juan J. Linz, "Comparative Perspectives on Inequality

and the Quality of Democracy in the United States," *Perspectives on Politics* 9, no. 4 (December 2011): 941–56.

36 Organisation for Economic Co-operation and Development, "Growing Unequal? Income Distribution and Poverty in OECD Countries," 2008, http://www.oecd.org/els/soc/growingunequalincomedistributionandpovertyin oecdcountries.htm.

37 Social Security and Medicare payroll taxes are formally known as Federal Insurance Contribution Act (FICA) taxes. In 2013, the FICA tax was 12.4 percent for Social Security (the employee and the employer each pay 6.2 percent) on wages up to $113,700, plus 2.9 percent for Medicare (the employee and the employer each pay 1.45 percent) on all wages. Beginning in 2013, an additional Medicare tax of 0.9 percent is paid by individuals whose wages exceed $200,000, part of the funding for the Patient Protection and Affordable Care Act of 2010. Employers pay into the UI and workers' compensation systems. US Social Security Administration, "Social Security and Medicare Tax Rates; Maximum Taxable Earnings," updated September 12, 2013, http://ssa-custhelp.ssa.gov/app/answers/detail/a_id/240.

38 In 2011, 31 percent of physicians would not accept new Medicaid patients, double the share refusing new Medicare patients; the lower the Medicaid-to-Medicare fee ratio in a state, the lower the Medicaid acceptance rate. See Sandra L. Decker, "In 2011 Nearly One-Third of Physicians Said They Would Not Accept New Medicaid Patients, but Rising Fees May Help," *Health Affairs* 31, no. 8 (August 2012): 1673–79.

39 See General Accounting Office, "Means-Tested Programs: Determining Financial Eligibility Is Cumbersome and Can Be Simplified," November 2001, http://www.gao.gov/new.items/d0258.pdf.

40 Some seniors with low incomes or weak work histories remain poor enough to qualify for SSI in addition to Social Security.

41 For example, a retired sixty-eight-year-old who last worked in 2012 and earned $25,000 would receive a monthly benefit in January 2014 of $1,152, for a "replacement rate" of 55 percent of earned wages. If the same person instead earned $100,000 in 2012, her monthly benefit would be $2,661, for a replacement rate of 32 percent. The higher earner's retirement benefit is larger absolutely, but replaces a smaller proportion of preretirement earnings. Actual retirement benefits would depend on the worker's precise earning history over time; these estimates are from the Social Security Administration's "Quick Calculator" and assume the worker's earnings have grown at the same pace as national average wages. Calculator available at http://

www.socialsecurity.gov/OACT/quickcalc/index.html, accessed February 28, 2014.

42 US Census Bureau, Current Population Survey, "Poverty Rates by Age: 1959 to 2011," September 17, 2013, http://www.census.gov/hhes/www/poverty/data/incpovhlth/2011/figure5.pdf.

43 In 2013, Medicare enrollees who were hospitalized had to pay a deductible of $1,184 for each hospital stay, plus daily coinsurance of $296 per day for days 61 to 90 and $592 per day for days 91 to 150. An enrollee who had a stay in a skilled nursing facility (for example, a rehab hospital stay after an acute hospitalization) had to pay daily coinsurance of $148 for days 21 to 100. For Medicare Part B, which covers doctors' visits, seniors paid an annual deductible of $147 and a $104.90 monthly premium on incomes up to $85,000 for individuals or $170,000 for couples. The premiums rose with income, up to a top monthly premium of $335.70 for individuals whose incomes exceeded $214,000 and couples with incomes above $428,000. Seniors also had to pay 20 percent coinsurance for doctors' visits and services and for any Medicare-covered medical equipment. If seniors had prescription drug coverage, they were required to pay a monthly premium and perhaps deductibles and co-payments for drugs as well. There has been no limit on these out-of-pocket costs, which for a small share of Medicare recipients can reach catastrophic levels. The 1987 Medicare Catastrophic Coverage Act sought to cap Medicare out-of-pocket costs, but it proved unpopular with seniors (who had to pay for the new benefit through higher monthly premiums and a tax surcharge on the richest 40 percent of seniors, even though most would never experience such catastrophic costs) and was repealed in 1988. On the MCCA, see Richard Himelfarb, *Catastrophic Politics: The Rise and Fall of the Medicare Catastrophic Coverage Act of 1988* (University Park, PA: Pennsylvania State University Press, 1995).

44 If you become disabled before the age of 24, to qualify for SSDI you have to have paid into the system (worked and paid payroll taxes) in 6 quarters during the three-year period ending when the disability begins. Between ages 24 and 30, you need to have worked and paid into the system about half the quarters between the age of 21 and the date of disability. If you are 31 or older, the number of quarters of work is scaled to your age (at age 45, 24 quarters are needed; at age 61 or older, 40 quarters are needed), and at least 20 of those quarters must have occurred within the ten years (40 quarters) immediately before the date of disability.

45 SSDI is not paid for partial or short-term disability—only total disability.

The definition: "You cannot do work that you did before; we decide that you cannot adjust to other work because of your medical condition(s); and your disability has lasted or is expected to last for at least one year or to result in death." US Social Security Administration, "Disability Planner: What We Mean by Disability," accessed February 28, 2014, http://www.ssa.gov/dibplan/dqualify4.htm.

46 Ted Robbins, "Arizona Budget Cuts Put Organ Transplants at Risk," National Public Radio, November 17, 2010, available at http://www.npr.org/2010/11/11/131215308/arizona-budget-cuts-put-organ-transplants-at-risk; Harold Pollack, "Hey, Lame-Duck Congress! Fix the Awful Medicare Waiting Period for Disabled People," *New Republic* Jonathan Cohn blog, November 18, 2010, http://www.newrepublic.com/blog/jonathan-cohn/79266/hey-lame-duck-congress-fix-the-awful-medicare-waiting-period-disabled-peopl.

47 Those with insurance were typically covered by a spouse's employer-based insurance, veterans' health benefits, or continued insurance from a former employer under the Consolidated Omnibus Budget Reconciliation Act, which allows qualified individuals to buy into their former employer's health insurance at the group rate for up to 18 months, as long as they pay the entire premium. See Stacy Berg Dale and James M. Verdier, "Elimination of Medicare's Waiting Period for Seriously Disabled Adults: Impact on Coverage and Costs," Commonwealth Fund, July 2003, http://www.commonwealthfund.org/usr_doc/660_Dale_elimination.pdf?section=4039. The same study found that dropping the waiting period would add approximately 3.4 percent to Medicare spending (at 2002 program levels), although it also would decrease Medicaid spending, because about 40 percent of SSDI recipients are covered by Medicaid during the waiting period (overall, federal Medicare spending would have been $8.7 billion higher for 2002, but federal Medicaid spending would have fallen by $2.5 billion, and state Medicaid spending would have fallen by $1.8 billion).

48 Hannah Shaw and Chad Stone, "Introduction to Unemployment Insurance," Center on Budget and Policy Priorities, June 25, 2012, http://www.cbpp.org/files/12-19-02ui.pdf. Furthermore, UI benefits are time-limited, small in size, and taxable. UI is a federal-state program, and in most states, UI benefits are limited to twenty-six weeks. When state economic conditions are poor, however, an Extended Benefit program can be triggered, and Congress has periodically extended federal unemployment benefits during recessions. For example, the American Recovery and Reinvestment Act of 2009 (the "stimulus bill" passed during the Great Recession) extended federal UI benefits up to ninety-nine weeks for some people. Many states try to provide fifty cents on the dollar, but benefits are generally capped, so that the "replace-

ment rate" is lower for higher earners. And across states, benefit levels vary dramatically.

49 Christopher Howard, "Workers' Compensation, Federalism, and the Heavy Hand of History," *Studies in American Political Development* 16 (Spring 2002): 28–47.

50 The private welfare state began in 1875 when the American Express Company offered the first private pension plan. Fringe benefits became more common during World War II, when the government imposed wage and price controls to stave off inflation. Because employers could no longer compete for employees with wages alone, they began to offer additional benefits, with health insurance—created only a few short years earlier, with the emergence of Blue Cross and Blue Shield during the 1930s—proving particularly popular. IRS rulings during the 1950s stipulating that health insurance and retirement plan contributions would not be taxed codified this system. See Paul Starr, *The Social Transformation of American Medicine* (New York: Basic Books, 1982).

51 Employee Benefit Research Institute, *EBRI Databook on Employee Benefits*, March 2011, http://www.ebri.org/pdf/publications/books/databook/DB.Chapter %2001.pdf, chapter 1.

52 US Bureau of Labor Statistics National Compensation Survey data cited in Kimberly J. Morgan, "America's Misguided Approach to Social Welfare," *Foreign Affairs*, January/February 2013, 157.

53 The share of the nonelderly population with employer-provided health insurance fell from 69 percent in 2000 to 58 percent in 2011. See Paul Fronstin, "Sources of Health Insurance and Characteristics of the Uninsured: Analysis of the March 2012 Current Population Survey," Employee Benefit Research Institute Issue Brief no. 376, September 2012, http://www.ebri.org/publications/ib/index.cfm?fa=ibDisp&content_id=5114.

54 Thanks to Frank Thompson for this point.

55 Essentially, retirement coverage has flipped: the proportion of private-sector workers participating solely in a traditional defined benefit plan fell from 62 percent in 1975 to 7 percent in 2009; conversely, the proportion of private-sector workers participating in a new-style defined contribution plan in which the DC was the only plan increased from 16 to 67 percent over the same period. See Fronstin, "Sources of Health Insurance and Characteristics of the Uninsured."

56 On tax expenditures as social policy, see Christopher Howard, *The Hidden Welfare State: Tax Expenditures and Social Policy in the United States* (Princeton, NJ: Princeton University Press, 1997); Howard, *The Welfare State Nobody*

Knows; and Suzanne Mettler, *The Submerged State: How Invisible Government Policies Undermine American Democracy* (Chicago: University of Chicago Press, 2011).

57 About 80 percent of total tax expenditures are in the individual income tax system, the other 20 percent in the corporate tax side.

58 In 2011, households in the top income quintile received two-thirds of all tax expenditure benefits. See also Congressional Budget Office, "The Distribution of Major Tax Expenditures in the Individual Income Tax System," May 2013, http://www.cbo.gov/sites/default/files/cbofiles/attachments/43768_ DistributionTaxExpenditures.pdf. One reason is that only one-third of tax expenditures are credits, in which the size of the break is the same regardless of income. Most are deductions from taxable income, the value of which rise at higher incomes in higher tax brackets. A family paying $5,000 in home mortgage interest gets a $1,750 tax break if they are in the 35 percent tax bracket, but only a $500 break if they are in the 10 percent bracket (and they must itemize deductions to get the break, which most low- and moderate-income families do not do). That the affluent receive most of the benefits of the tax expenditure system undercuts the progressivity of the federal income tax, which in turn reduces the progressivity of the overall tax system.

Indeed, the reduced progressivity of the income tax, combined with a number of other taxes in the American system that are regressive or flat, results in a nearly flat overall tax system. For example, the Social Security payroll tax, which all workers pay, is regressive, falling more heavily on low earners (employees paid 6.2 percent of their earnings into the system on the first $113,700 in 2013, but there is no tax above that earnings level). State sales taxes are regressive also; everyone pays the same rate on purchases, but lower-income people spend a greater portion of their income than do higher-income people, so sales taxes consume a greater share of their incomes. The Medicare payroll tax is flat (1.45 percent on all earnings, although high earners pay a little more under the ACA). Income taxes in many states are flat as well. Taking federal, state, and local taxes together, the system is virtually flat, with each income group's share of total taxes paid equaling its share of total income. In 2011, the lowest fifth of earners received 3.4 percent of total income and paid 2.1 percent of total taxes. The middle fifth received 11.4 percent of income and paid 10.3 percent of taxes. And the top 1 percent received 21 percent of income and paid 21.6 percent of all taxes (see Institute on Taxation and Economic Policy Tax Model, April 2012, cited in Chuck Marr and Chye-Ching Huang, "Misconceptions and Realities about Who Pays

Taxes," Center on Budget and Policy Priorities, September 17, 2012, http://www.cbpp.org/files/5-26-11tax.pdf, p. 7). In sum, the American tax system is not very progressive. When combined with social programs that exclude large proportions of people in need and that give small benefits to those who do qualify, the result is relatively little redistribution of income from high- to low-income households—and much higher poverty levels—compared with other rich nations.

59 Benjamin H. Harris and Daniel Baneman, "Who Itemizes Deductions?," *Tax Notes*, January 17, 2011, 345.

60 Julie Turkewitz and Juliet Linderman, "The Disability Trap," *New York Times*, October 21, 2012.

61 The $1,267 SSDI benefit amount comes from entering Dave's birthday and pre-accident salary into the Social Security Administration's "Quick Calculator," accessed February 28, 2014, http://www.socialsecurity.gov/OACT/quickcalc/index.html.

62 The other states with short-term disability insurance are Rhode Island, New Jersey, New York, and Hawaii. Marcella does not qualify for California's short-term disability program because she was not a worker. California's and New Jersey's state-paid family leave programs operate out of their state disability insurance funds. See State of California, "State Disability Insurance Program" fact sheet, accessed February 28, 2014, http://www.edd.ca.gov/pdf_pub_ctr/de8714c.pdf.

63 In 1986, the COBRA health benefit provision was instituted, which allows those who have lost their jobs to continue to buy into their employers' health insurance plan for up to eighteen months at the group rate, which is typically far less than the cost of health insurance on the individual market. The catch is that the former employer must pay the entire cost of the insurance. Without the employer subsidy, many people can't afford even the group rate insurance. For example, my four-person family gets HMO coverage through my husband's employer for which we paid $6,021 in 2013. His employer paid $14,049. If my husband and I were to lose our jobs and needed to use COBRA to remain covered, we would have to pay the entire $20,070 premium ourselves ($1,673 per month).

64 On Medicaid as a middle-class program, see Colleen M. Grogan and Eric Patashnik, "Universalism within Targeting: Nursing Home Care, the Middle Class, and the Politics of the Medicaid Program," *Social Service Review* 77, no. 1 (March 2003): 51–71; and Colleen M. Grogan, "Medicaid: Health Care for You and Me?," in *Health Politics and Policy*, ed. James Morone, Theodor Litman, and Leonard Robins, 2nd. ed. (New York: Delmar Thompson, 2012).

65 US Department of Health and Human Services, Centers for Medicare and Medicaid Services, "Medicare and Other Health Benefits: Your Guide to Who Pays First," November 2011, http://www.medicare.gov/Pubs/pdf/02179.pdf.

66 Robin Marantz Henig, "A Life-or-Death Situation," *New York Times Sunday Magazine*, July 21, 2013, 29.

67 Kelly Greene and Leslie Scism, "Long-Term-Care Insurance Gap Hits Seniors," *Wall Street Journal*, July 1, 2013, http://online.wsj.com/news/articles/SB10001424127887323475304578501820197828966. When the value of informal caregiving is included in the total, private LTC insurance funds only 1 percent of all LTC spending in the United States. See "The State of Long-Term Care Financing," Scan Foundation, accessed February 28, 2014, http://www.thescanfoundation.org/briefing-whats-state-ltc-financing-and-what-are-options-future.

68 Michael Ogg, "Planning for the Long Term: Taking Action Today," National Multiple Sclerosis Society blog, May 20, 2013, http://blog.nationalmssociety.org/2013/05/planning-for-long-term-taking-action.html. Also, personal interview, April 23, 2013; and Michael Ogg, "Running Out of Time, Money, and Independence?," *Health Affairs* 30, no. 1 (January 2011): 173–76.

69 Thanks to Harold Pollack for this point.

70 Joe Soss, "Making Clients and Citizens: Welfare Policy as a Source of Status, Belief, and Action," in *Deserving and Entitled: Social Constructions and Public Policy*, ed. Anne L. Schneider and Helen M. Ingram (Albany: State University of New York Press, 2005), 327.

CHAPTER FOUR

1 Many thanks to Joe Soss for helping me understand the relationships among these systems.

2 Julia Lynch, "A Cross-National Perspective on the American Welfare State," in *Oxford Handbook of Social Policy*, ed. Daniel Béland, Christopher Howard, and Kimberly Morgan (Oxford: Oxford University Press); this article now available online for downloading as of January 2014, accessed March 5, 2014, at http://www.oxfordhandbooks.com/view/10.1093/oxfordhb/9780199838509.001.0001/oxfordhb-9780199838509-e-023.

3 Euromonitor International, "World Consumer Income & Expenditure Patterns 2012," table 3.5, "Disposable Income per Household," 48, http://www.euromonitor.com/medialibrary/PDF/Book_WCIEP.pdf.

4 In the median state, the two benefits together come to 57 percent of the poverty line, ranging from 45 percent in Mississippi to 70 percent in New York, still far below the poverty line. See US House Ways and Means Commit-

tee, *2011 Greenbook*, greenbook.waysandmeans.house.gov/2011-green-book/chapter-7-temporary-assistance-for-needy-families/tanf-tables-and-figures, table 7–25.

5 US Social Security Administration, Annual Statistical Supplement, 2012, "Supplemental Security Income," table 7.A1, http://www.ssa.gov/policy/docs/statcomps/supplement/2012/7a.html.

6 Suzanne Mettler and Andrew Milstein, "American Political Development from the Citizens' Perspective: Tracking Federal Government's Presence in Individual Lives over Time," *Studies in American Political Development* 21, no. 1 (March 2007): 110–30. On political polarization in Congress preventing the constant updating that policies like the minimum wage require, see Nolan M. McCarty, Keith T. Poole, and Howard Rosenthal, *Polarized America: The Dance of Ideology and Unequal Riches* (Cambridge, MA: MIT Press, 2006).

7 Heather Hahn, Olivia Golden, and Peter Edelman, "Strengthening TANF for States and Needy Families," Urban Institute, August 22, 2012, http://www.urban.org/UploadedPDF/412636-Strengthening-TANF-for-States-and-Needy-Families.pdf.

8 US Department of Health and Human Services, Low-Income Home Energy Assistance Program brochure, November 1, 2009, http://www.acf.hhs.gov/programs/ocs/resource/liheap-brochures.

9 Center on Budget and Policy Priorities, "Federal Rental Assistance," January 25, 2013, http://www.cbpp.org/cms/?fa=view&id=3890.

10 Edward G. Goetz, *New Deal Ruins: Race, Economic Justice, and Public Housing Policy* (Ithaca, NY: Cornell University Press, 2013), 177.

11 Mireya Navarro, "227,000 Names on List Vie for Rare Vacancies in City's Public Housing," *New York Times*, July 24, 2013.

12 Thanks to Harold Pollack for this characterization.

13 Barbara Ehrenreich, *Nickel and Dimed: On (Not) Getting by in America* (New York: Metropolitan Books, 2001).

14 Personal communication, June 19, 2013.

15 Aleta Sprague, "Lifting the Medicaid Asset Test: A Step in the Right Direction," New America Foundation, April 9, 2012, http://assets.newamerica.net/blogposts/2012/lifting_the_medicaid_asset_test_a_step_in_the_right_direction-66214.

16 Signe-Mary McKernan, Caroline Ratcliffe, and Katie Vinopal, "Do Assets Help Families Cope with Adverse Events?," Urban Institute, December 14, 2009, http://www.urban.org/UploadedPDF/411994_help_family_cope.pdf. See also Alejandra Lopez-Fernandini, "Unrestricted Savings: Their Roles in Household Economic Security and the Case for Policy Action," New America

Foundation, 2010, http://assets.newamerica.net/sites/newamerica.net/files/policydocs/UnrestrictedSavingsWorkingPaper.pdf.

17 Reid Cramer, Rourke O'Brien, Daniel Cooper, and Maria Luengo-Prado, "A Penny Saved Is Mobility Earned: Advancing Economic Mobility through Savings," Pew Economic Mobility Project, 2009, http://www.pewtrusts.org/uploadedFiles/wwwpewtrustsorg/Reports/Economic_Mobility/EMP_Savings_Report.pdf.

18 Julie Turkewitz and Juliet Linderman, "The Disability Trap," *New York Times*, October 21, 2012.

19 C. Eugene Steuerle, "Marginal Tax Rates, Work, and the Nation's Real Tax System," testimony before the Joint Hearing of the Human Resources and the Select Revenue Measures Subcommittees of the US House Ways and Means Committee, June 27, 2012, http://www.urban.org/UploadedPDF/901508-Marginal-Tax-Rates-Work-and-the-Nations-Real-Tax-System.pdf.

20 Ibid., 10.

21 Kathryn Edin and Laura Lein, *Making Ends Meet: How Single Mothers Survive Welfare and Low-Wage Work* (New York: Russell Sage Foundation, 1997), 109–19. On quality concerns and other shortcomings of day care, especially that available to lower-income families, see Jonathan Cohn, "The Hell of American Day Care," *New Republic*, April 15, 2013, 22–27.

22 Which continues to be true even after the enactment of the Affordable Care Act, since half the states choose not to expand Medicaid to cover all poor people under 138 percent of the federal poverty line. See chapter 6.

23 Joe Soss, Richard C. Fording, and Sanford F. Schram, *Disciplining the Poor: Neoliberal Paternalism and the Persistent Power of Race* (Chicago: University of Chicago Press, 2011).

24 Personal interview, April 30, 2013.

25 Turkewitz and Linderman, "The Disability Trap."

26 See Oscar Lewis, *Five Families: Mexican Case Studies in the Culture of Poverty* (New York: Basic Books, 1959), and his "The Culture of Poverty," *Scientific American* 215, no. 4 (October 1966): 19–25. The culture of poverty concept also figures in other influential work of the period, such as Michael Harrington, *The Other America* (New York: Macmillan, 1962), and Daniel Patrick Moynihan, "The Negro Family: The Case of National Action," Office of Policy Planning and Research, Department of Labor (Washington, DC: Government Printing Office, 1965).

27 Stuart M. Butler, "Can the American Dream Be Saved," *National Affairs* 14 (Winter 2013): 45; italics in the original.

28 See Robert A. Moffitt, "The Great Recession and the Social Safety Net," *Annals of the American Academy of Political and Social Science* 650 (2013): 143–66.

29 Steuerle, "Marginal Tax Rates," 11.

30 Some states allow Individual Development Accounts, special savings accounts for low- and moderate-income people with earned income (generally below 200 percent of the federal poverty level) in which their savings are matched for a two- or three-year period (in some states, TANF money can be used to match the savings of welfare recipients). The savings are meant for a specific goal, such as education, job training, home purchase, or business start-up. Participants typically have to take a financial literacy course by a sponsoring organization (either a bank or a nonprofit organization). State policy decides whether an individual in a means-tested program with an asset limit can participate. Economist Michael Sherraden developed the idea during the 1980s. See his *Assets and the Poor: A New American Welfare Policy* (Armonk, NY: M. E. Sharpe, 1991). Also see Andrew Karch, *Democratic Laboratories: Policy Diffusion among the American States* (Ann Arbor: University of Michigan Press, 2007), and World Institute on Disability, "Individual Development Account Question and Answer Sheet: A Guide for IDA Consumers with Disabilities," accessed February 28, 2014, http://www.wid.org/publications/individual-development-account-question-and-answer-sheet-a-guide-for-ida-consumers-with-disabilities/.

31 Theda Skocpol, *The Missing Middle: Working Families and the Future of American Social Policy* (New York: W. W. Norton, 2000).

32 Eileen Appelbaum and Ruth Milkman, "Paid Family Leave Pays Off in California," Harvard Business Review HBR Blog Network/Research, January 19, 2011, http://blogs.hbr.org/research/2011/01/paid-family-leave-pays-off-in.html. Also, Ruth Milkman and Eileen Appelbaum, *Unfinished Business: Paid Family Leave in California and the Future of U.S. Work-Family Policy* (Ithaca, NY: Cornell University Press, 2013).

33 Lane Kenworthy's list of needed social protections includes true universal health insurance, paid family leave, an increased and indexed minimum wage, and increased EITC and Child Tax Credits, among others. See *Social Democratic America* (New York: Oxford University Press, 2014).

CHAPTER FIVE

1 Rourke O'Brien, "529s and Public Assistance: Asset Limits as a Barrier to College Savings," New American Foundation, November 2009, http://newamerica.net/publications/policy/529s_and_public_assistance.

2 Christopher Howard, "The American Welfare State, or States?," *Political Research Quarterly* 52, no. 2 (June 1999): 421–42.

3 On the origins on New Deal programs and the role of race, see Robert C. Lieberman, *Shifting the Color Line: Race and the American Welfare State* (Cambridge, MA: Harvard University Press, 1998); Jill Quadagno, *The Color of Welfare: How Racism Undermined the War on Poverty* (New York: Oxford University Press, 1994); and Ira Katznelson, *Fear Itself: The New Deal and the Origins of Our Time* (New York: Liveright, 2013), on which this section is based. On gender and the New Deal, see Suzanne Mettler, *Dividing Citizens: Gender and Federalism in New Deal Public Policy* (Ithaca, NY: Cornell University Press, 1998).

4 Theda Skocpol, *Protecting Soldiers and Mothers: The Political Origins of Social Policy in the United States* (Cambridge, MA: Harvard University Press, 1992), 471–72; Lieberman, *Shifting the Color Line*, 37.

5 Lieberman, *Shifting the Color Line*, 27.

6 Social Security covered only half the American workforce at the beginning because it excluded many occupations; collecting payroll taxes from commercial and industrial employees was considered easiest administratively. Excluded occupations included professionals, employees of nonprofits, the self-employed, and others. See Larry DeWitt, "The Decision to Exclude Agricultural and Domestic Workers from the 1935 Social Security Act," *Social Security Bulletin* 70, no. 4 (2010).

7 Lieberman, *Shifting the Color Line*, 51.

8 On Medicare's development, see Theodore R. Marmor, *The Politics of Medicare* (Chicago: Aldine, 1973); Jonathan Oberlander, *The Political Life of Medicare* (Chicago: University of Chicago Press, 2003); and Kimberly J. Morgan and Andrea Louise Campbell, *The Delegated Welfare State: Medicare, Markets, and the Governance of Social Policy* (New York: Oxford University Press, 2011). On Medicaid's development and the goals of its framers, see Jonathan Engel, *Poor People's Medicine: Medicaid and American Charity Care since 1965* (Durham, NC: Duke University Press, 2006); Colleen M. Grogan and Michael K. Gusmano, *Healthy Voices, Unhealthy Silence: Advocacy and Health Policy for the Poor* (Washington, DC: Georgetown University Press, 2007); David G. Smith and Judith D. Moore, *Medicaid Politics and Policy: 1965–2007* (New Brunswick, NJ: Transaction, 2008); Katherine Swartz, "Health Care for the Poor: For Whom, What Care, and Whose Responsibility?," in *Changing Poverty, Changing Policies*, ed. Maria Cancian and Sheldon Danziger (New York: Russell Sage Foundation, 2009), 330–64; and Laura Katz Olson, *The Politics of Medicaid* (New York: Columbia University Press, 2010).

9 Martin Gilens, *Why Americans Hate Welfare: Race, Media and the Politics of Anti-*

poverty Policy (Chicago: University of Chicago Press, 1999); Thomas Byrne Edsall and Mary D. Edsall, *Chain Reaction: The Impact of Race, Rights and Taxes on American Politics* (New York: W. W. Norton, 1991); Sanford F. Schram, Joe Soss, and Richard C. Fording, eds., *Race and the Politics of Welfare Reform* (Ann Arbor: University of Michigan Press, 2003); and Joe Soss, Richard C. Fording, and Sanford F. Schram, *Disciplining the Poor: Neoliberal Paternalism and the Persistent Power of Race* (Chicago: University of Chicago Press, 2011).

10 US House Ways and Means Committee, *2011 Greenbook*, http://greenbook .waysandmeans.house.gov/2011-green-book/chapter-7-temporary -assistance-for-needy-families/tanf-tables-and-figures, table 7-9.

11 Urban Institute, "Welfare Rules Databook: State TANF Policies as of July 2011," August 2012, table II.A.4, 90–91, http://www.urban.org/publications/412641 .html.

12 Sixty-six percent of Ethiopians, 82 percent of Rwandans, and 87 percent of Zambians live on $2 per day. World Bank, "Poverty Headcount Ratio at $2 per Day," accessed February 28, 2014, http://data.worldbank.org/indicator/ SI.POV.2DAY.

13 I divided the maximum TANF benefit for a family of three by the Economic Policy Institute's Family Budget Calculator result for a one-adult, two-child family in the largest city in each state. The result is a measure of adequacy that accounts for differences in the cost of living. Economic Policy Institute, "Family Budget Calculator," accessed February 28, 2014, http://www.epi.org/ resources/budget/.

14 Urban Institute, "Welfare Rules Databook," table I.C.1, 58–60.

15 Ibid., table I.A.1, 32–35.

16 Ibid., table I.A.2, 36–40.

17 Ibid., tables I.D.2 and I.D.1, 62–65.

18 Congressional Research Service, "Temporary Assistance for Needy Families (TANF): Welfare-to-Work Revisited," October 2, 2012, Report T42767, https:// www.fas.org/sgp/crs/misc/R42768.pdf.

19 TANF program sanctions have become more severe. In 1997, only 1 state would close a family's case entirely as the ultimate sanction for failing to comply with the work requirement, while another 9 would reduce family benefits to $0 temporarily. By 2009, 21 states would close the case entirely, and another 24 would reduce benefits to $0. See ibid., 47–48. Also note that TANF permits a benefits cutoff for the entire family; before TANF, sanctions could only reduce or eliminate the adults' portion of cash assistance but not the children's portion.

20 Fay Lomax Cook and Edith J. Barrett, *Support for the American Welfare State:*

The Views of Congress and the Public (New York: Columbia University Press, 1992), 62.

21 Ibid.; Daniel Carpenter, "Is Health Politics Different?," *Annual Review of Political Science* 15 (2012): 287–311.

22 On Medicaid's early years and the origins of interstate variation in eligibility and benefits, see chapter 3 of Michael S. Sparer, *Medicaid and the Limits of State Health Reform* (Philadelphia: Temple University Press, 1996), 31–65.

23 Kaiser Commission on Medicaid and the Uninsured, "Performing under Pressure: Annual Findings of a 50-State Survey of Eligibility, Enrollment, Renewal, and Cost-Sharing Policies in Medicaid and CHIP, 2011–2012," January 2012, 45, http://www.kff.org/medicaid/upload/8272.pdf.

24 Kaiser Commission on Medicaid and the Uninsured, "Medicaid in a Historic Time of Transformation: Results from a 50-State Medicaid Budget Survey for State Fiscal Years 2013 and 2014," October 2013, http://kaiserfamily foundation.files.wordpress.com/2013/10/8498-medicaid-in-a-historic-time4 .pdf, 10.

25 Section 529 plans, named for a section of the federal tax code, are a means to save for a child's college education; as of 2002, investment gains are not taxed, and as long as the funds are used for the child's qualified educational costs, there are no taxes on the withdrawals. Their tax-free nature has made them popular. In twelve states, such plans are not counted against the Medicaid asset test, but in twenty-four states, including California, they are. Note also that 529 plans can threaten Medicaid benefits for family members making the contributions. For example, if a grandparent opens and funds a 529 plan for a grandchild's education, those funds may be considered an "available asset" if the grandparent needs long-term care and wishes to go on Medicaid. And then not only does the money fail to benefit the child as intended, but also spending the money on long-term care rather than education would trigger deferred taxes plus penalties of 10 percent (20 percent in some states). A grandparent could transfer the funds to another relative such as the child's parents, but would need to do so before the Medicaid look-back period. See Elderly Law Answers, "529 Plan Assets Can Collide with Medicaid Eligibility," accessed February 28, 2014, http://www.elderlaw answers.com/Resources/Article.asp?ID=2299.

26 US Department of Health and Human Services, Centers for Medicare and Medicaid Services, Medicaid.gov, "Medicaid Benefits," accessed February 28, 2014, http://www.medicaid.gov/Medicaid-CHIP-Program-Information/ By-Topics/Benefits/Medicaid-Benefits.html.

27 Congressional Research Service, "Prescription Drug Coverage under Med-

icaid," February 6, 2008, http://www.aging.senate.gov/crs/medicaid16.pdf. Taming prescription drug costs has been the focus of much state innovation. See National Conference of State Legislatures, "Recent Medicaid Prescription Drug Laws and Strategies, 2001–2012," accessed February 28, 2014, http://www.ncsl.org/issues-research/health/medicaid-pharmaceutical-laws -and-policies.aspx.

28 As of 2007, 6 states provide no dental coverage to adults, 16 provide emergency services only, and 13 offer limited coverage (excluding root canals or crowns, for example). See Mary McGinn-Shapiro, "Medicaid Coverage of Adult Dental Services," National Academy for State Health Policy, October 2008, http://www.nashp.org/sites/default/files/Adult%20Dental%20 Monitor.pdf.

29 US Department of Health and Human Services, Centers for Medicare and Medicaid Services, Medicaid.gov, "Medicaid Benefits."

30 Kaiser Commission on Medicaid and the Uninsured, "Medicaid Financing: An Overview of the Federal Medicaid Assistance Matching Rate (FMAP)," Policy Brief, Publication #8352, September 2012, www.kff.org/kcmu.

31 John Holahan, "State Variation in Medicaid Spending: Hard to Justify," *Health Affairs* Web Exclusive, September 18, 2007, http://content.health affairs.org/ content/26/6/w667.abstract, W667–69; Swartz, "Health Care for the Poor."

32 Unless otherwise stated, the benefits cited in this paragraph are from Kaiser Family Foundation, "State Health Facts, Medicaid Benefits," October 1, 2010, http://kff.org/data-collection/medicaid-benefits/.

33 MassHealth Dental Program, accessed February 28, 2014, http://www.mass resources.org/masshealth-dental.html.

34 Aleta Sprague, "Lifting the Medicaid Asset Test: A Step in the Right Direction," New American Foundation, April 9, 2012, http://assets.newamerica .net/blogposts/2012/lifting_the_medicaid_asset_test_a_step_in_the_right _direction-66214.

35 The ratio of the highest to lowest state CHIP income limit is 2.5 to 1 (New York to North Dakota), but the greatest cost-of-living difference across the country (New York to Mississippi) is only 1.9 to 1, as calculated from the Economic Policy Institute's Family Budget Calculator.

36 Kaiser Family Foundation, "Performing under Pressure: Annual Findings of a 50-State Survey of Eligibility, Enrollment, Renewal, and Cost-Sharing Policies in Medicaid and CHIP, 2011–12," January 2012, http://www.kff.org/ medicaid/upload/8272.pdf, table 1A.

37 Kaiser Family Foundation, Statehealthfacts.org, November 14, 2013, http:// kff.org/statedata/.

38 Medicare Matters Maryland, "Background on the CHIP Waiting Period Issue and Suggested Talking Points: Kids Shouldn't Have to Wait for Coverage," April 10, 2013, http://www.medicaidmattersmd.org/mmmd-members.html.

39 This section is drawn from Nicholas Johnson and Erica Williams, "A Hand Up: How State Earned Income Tax Credits Help Working Families Escape Poverty in 2011," Center on Budget and Policy Priorities, April 2011, http://www.cbpp.org/cms/?fa=view&id=3474.

40 James P. Ziliak, "Understanding Poverty Rates and Gaps: Concepts, Trends, and Challenges," *Foundations and Trends in Microeconomics* 1, no. 3: 127–99.

41 With the creation of state EITCs, the number of states imposing income taxes on poor workers dropped from 21 to 11 (taxing poor single parents) and from 26 to 13 (taxing poor couples). Johnson and Williams, "A Hand Up," 12.

42 States also vary as to whether the credit is "refundable." In most states it is—which means that workers can receive a credit greater than their state income tax liability. In three states it is not, however, and in one state (Rhode Island) it is only partially refundable.

43 US Social Security Administration, "State Assistance Programs for SSI Recipients, January 2011," http://www.ssa.gov/policy/docs/progdesc/ssi_st_asst/2011/ssi_st_asst2011.pdf.

44 US Social Security Administration, "Nutrition Assistance Programs," SSA Publication no. 05-10100, ICN 468650, August 2011, http://www.ssa.gov/pubs/10100.html#a0=0.

45 US Social Security Administration, "Supplemental Security Income (SSI) in California," SSA Publication no. 05-11125, January 2012, http://www.social security.gov/pubs/11125.html#a0=4.

46 US Social Security Administration, "Supplemental Security Income (SSI) in Massachusetts," SSA Publication no. 05-11130, January 2012, http://www.ssa.gov/pubs/11130.html#a0=2; US Department of Agriculture, "Supplemental Nutrition Assistance Program: Average Monthly Benefit Per Person," November 8, 2013, http://www.fns.usda.gov/pd/18SNAPavg$PP.htm.

47 Karen C. Cunnyngham, Laura A. Castner, and Allen L. Schirm, "Reaching Those in Need: State Food Stamp Participation Rates in 2006," Mathematica Policy Research, November 2008, http://www.mathematica-mpr.com/publications/pdfs/fns06rates.pdf. The report does take into the account the fact that SSI recipients are ineligible for food stamps in California.

48 In late 2013, Rhode Island passed a four-week paid family leave law. See Brigid Schulte, "States Make Moves toward Paid Family Leave," *Washington Post*, December 29, 2013, http://www.washingtonpost.com/local/states

-make-moves-toward-paid-family-leave/2013/12/29/568691ee-6297-11e3
-a373-0f9f2d1c2b61_story.html.

49 Kaiser Family Foundation, "State Health Facts, Medicaid Benefits: Personal Care Services," October 1, 2010, http://kff.org/medicaid/state-indicator/personal-care-services/. In this Kaiser chart, Tennessee is listed as providing no personal care assistance. In 2010, it secured a waiver to begin providing some home-based care. See State of Tennessee, "TennCare Launches CHOICES in Long-Term Care Program Statewide," August 2, 2010, https://news.tn.gov/node/5650.

50 Personal interview, May 17, 2013.

51 Noreen M. Glover-Graf, Michael Millington, and Irmo Marini, *Psychosocial Aspects of Disability: Insider Perspectives for Strategies for Counselors* (New York: Springer, 2011), 116.

52 Personal interview, December 5, 2013.

53 TennCare LTSS Governor's Dashboard Graphs, "LTC Enrollment by Calendar Year," accessed February 28, 2014, http://www.tn.gov/tenncare/long_graphs.shtml.

54 Ibid.

55 For references to the "underground railroad," see Tim Wheat, "America Needs to Reform Medicaid with S 971 and HR 2032, the Medicaid Community Attendant Services and Supports Act," ADAPT's Free Our People March, September 14, 2003, http://www.adapt.org/freeourpeople/reports/day11s.htm; and the ADAPT *Incitement* newsletter 22, no. 2 (Summer 2006), http://www.adapt.org/freeourpeople/adapt25/incitement/incit22-2.pdf. On ADAPT, see Doris Zames Fleischer and Frieda Zames, *The Disability Rights Movement: From Charity to Confrontation* (Philadelphia: Temple University Press, 2011), 82–85.

56 The following discussion is taken from John Holahan, Alan Weil, and Joshua M. Wiener, eds., *Federalism and Health Policy* (Washington, DC: Urban Institute Press, 2003), particularly chapter 1, "Federalism and Health Policy: An Overview," by John Holahan, Alan Weil, and Joshua M. Wiener, 1–23; and chapter 2, "State and Federal Roles in Health Care: Rationales for Allocating Responsibilities," by Randall R. Bovberg, Joshua M. Wiener, and Michael Housman, 25–57.

57 Thomas R. Dye, *American Federalism: Competition among Governments* (Lexington, MA: Lexington Books, 1990), 13–17.

58 The correlation between state poverty rate and Medicaid expenditures per poor person is −.54, while the correlation between state per capita income

and Medicaid expenditures is .66. Thus, richer states can afford to do more, and states with more poverty can afford to do less—the opposite of what the responsiveness argument would require. Frank J. Thompson, *Medicaid Politics: Federalism, Policy Durability, and Health Reform* (Washington, DC: Georgetown University Press, 2012), 222. Also, more conservative states (as measured by citizen ideology) spend less. See Donald J. Boyd, "Medicaid Devolution: A Fiscal Perspective," in *Medicaid and Devolution: A View from the States*, ed. Frank J. Thompson and John J. DiIulio Jr. (Washington, DC: Brookings Institution Press, 1998), 56–105, especially p. 90; and Charles J. Barrilleaux and Mark E. Miller, "The Political Economy of State Medicaid Policy," *American Political Science Review* 82, no. 4 (December 1988): 1089–1107.

59 Boyd, "Medicaid Devolution," 65–70.

60 Ibid., 66.

61 Health economists Thomas W. Grannemann and Mark Pauly have proposed a revised matching formula that incorporates some of these additional factors. See chapter 8, "Recommendations for Revising Federal Financing," in their book *Medicaid Everyone Can Count On: Public Choices for Equity and Efficiency* (Washington, DC: AEI Press, 2010), 156–76.

62 Renee Dudley, "SC Medicaid Cuts to Cripple Several Hospitals," *Post and Courier* (Charleston, SC), June 10, 2011, http://www.postandcourier.com/article/20110610/PC1602/306109916.

63 Nicholas Johnson, Phil Oliff, and Erica Williams, "An Update on State Budget Cuts," Center on Budget and Policy Priorities, February 9, 2011, http://www.cbpp.org/files/3-13-08sfp.pdf.

64 On the Great Recession exposing states' structural deficits and lack of fiscal capacity for social assistance, see Elizabeth McNichol, "Out of Balance: Cuts in Services Have Been States' Primary Response to Budget Gaps, Harming the Nation's Economy," Center of Budget and Policy Priorities, April 18, 2012, http://www.cbpp.org/files/4-18-12sfp.pdf.

65 On the point that arguments about responsiveness and innovation assume that people have different needs in different states (which is inaccurate when it comes to social programs, as discussed here), see Lisa L. Miller, "What's the Matter with American Politics? On Collective Action, Competition and Constraint," paper presented at the Department of Political Science, University of Texas, Austin, March 18, 2013.

66 Craig Volden, "States as Policy Laboratories: Emulating Success in the Children's Health Insurance Program," *American Journal of Political Science* 50, no. 2 (April 2006): 294–312.

67 David Shapiro, "Banking on Bondage: Private Prisons and Mass Incarcera-

tion," American Civil Liberties Union, November 2, 2011, accessed March 5, 2014, http://www.aclu.org/files/assets/bankingonbondage_20111102.pdf; and Cody Mason, "Too Good to Be True: Private Prisons in America," The Sentencing Project, January 2012, accessed March 5, 2014, http://sentencing project.org/doc/publications/inc_Too_Good_to_be_True.pdf.

68 See the perspectives offered in this *New York Times Room for Debate* conversation (December 2, 2009): http://roomfordebate.blogs.nytimes.com/2009/12/02/squeezing-money-out-of-home-health-care/?_r=2.

69 Personal interview, Dennis Heaphy, May 17, 2013. As of October 2012, thirty-four states reported that they were considering new payment or care delivery options for dual eligibles under the new Medicare-Medicaid Coordination Office established by the Affordable Care Act, but only Massachusetts had finalized a Memorandum of Understanding to move ahead on implementation (see "Medicaid Today; Preparing for Tomorrow: A Look at State Medicaid Program Spending, Enrollment and Policy Trends," Kaiser Commission on Medicaid and the Uninsured, October 2012, http://kff.org/medicaid/report/medicaid-today-preparing-for-tomorrow-a-look-at-state-medicaid-program-spending-enrollment-and-policy-trends-results-from-a-50-state-medicaid-budget-survey-for-state-fiscal-years-2012-and-2013/). The Massachusetts demonstration proposal is available at http://www.mass.gov/eohhs/docs/eohhs/healthcare-reform/prev-meetings/120216-final-proposal.pdf.

70 Deborah Stone, *Policy Paradox: The Art of Political Decision Making*, rev. ed. (New York: W. W. Norton, 2002), 61.

71 Paul E. Peterson, *The Price of Federalism* (Washington, DC: Brookings Institution Press, 1995), 27–30.

72 Debra Jasper and Spencer Hunt, "Fewer Doctors Willing to Treat Medicaid Patients," Extreme Choices Special Report, *Cincinnati Enquirer*, December 2003, accessed March 5, 2014, http://enquirer.com/extremechoices/loc_extremehavenots.html.

73 John Holahan, "Variation in Health Insurance Coverage and Medical Expenditures: How Much Is Too Much," in Holahan, Weil, and Wiener, *Federalism and Health Policy*, 111–43; the statement in the text is drawn from pp. 134–35.

74 Laura Snyder, Robin Rudowitz, Rachel Garfield, and Tracy Gordon, "Why Does Medicaid Spending Vary Across States: A Chart Book of Factors Driving State Spending," Kaiser Family Foundation, October 2012, http://kaiserfamily foundation.files.wordpress.com/2013/01/8378.pdf. See Michael S. Sparer's *Medicaid and the Limits of State Health Reform* (Philadelphia: Temple University Press, 1996) for an extensive study of Medicaid policy development in California and New York that explores why per recipient spending is so low

in the former and so high in the latter. A few factors: Medi-Cal was developed under the auspices of newly elected governor Ronald Reagan, who housed the program not in the Department of Social Welfare, which he perceived as a liberal social services bureaucracy, but in a newly created Department of Health Services headed by his appointees. Although the state legislature passed generous eligibility and benefit provisions, the DHS bureaucrats had control over provider reimbursement levels, which they set quite low. In addition, home health care workers in California were paid near-minimum wages, while in New York such workers were more likely to be represented by unions, which demanded higher pay. Sparer's thesis is that a strong, centralized bureaucracy held down costs in California, while in New York Medicaid policy was influenced more by powerful interest groups such as health care unions and hospital organizations, which successfully secured greater payments and a higher-cost program. Most of these differences persist.

75 Frank J. Thompson, *Medicaid Politics: Federalism, Policy Durability, and Health Reform* (Washington, DC: Georgetown University Press, 2012), 24.

76 Michael A. Bailey, "Welfare and the Multifaceted Decision to Move," *American Political Science Review* 99, no. 1 (February 2005): 125–35.

77 Holahan, Weil, and Wiener, "Federalism and Health Policy," 5–6.

78 Families USA, "CHIPRA 101: Overview of the CHIP Reauthorization Legislation," accessed February 28, 2014, http://familiesusa2.org/assets/pdfs/chipra/chipra-101-overview.pdf.

79 Thanks to Craig Volden for this term.

CHAPTER SIX

1 The Shasta County Office of Education website says that its Early Childhood Services are funded by a combination of federal, state, and county sources. See http://www.shastacoe.org/page.cfm?p=2481, accessed February 28, 2014.

2 Carol Stack, *All Our Kin* (New York: Basic Books, 1974); Kathryn Edin and Laura Lein, *Making Ends Meet: How Single Mothers Survive Welfare and Low-Wage Work* (New York: Russell Sage Foundation, 1997).

3 Alice Goffman, presentation at the annual meeting of the Robert Wood Johnson Scholars in Health Policy Research Program, Lansdowne, Virginia, May 30–June 1, 2012.

4 Bruce C. Vladeck, *Unloving Care: The Nursing Home Tragedy* (New York: Basic Books, 1980).

5 Kaiser Family Foundation, "Summary of New Health Reform Law," Publi-

cation no. 8061, April 25, 2011, http://www.kff.org/healthreform/upload/8061
.pdf.

6 The ACA eliminates the asset test for those newly eligible for Medicaid (this
   does not help Dave and Marcella, who are still under California's asset test because she is a member of a previously eligible group, the disabled). See Aleta
   Sprague, "Lifting the Medicaid Asset Test: A Step in the Right Direction," New
   America Foundation, April 9, 2012, http://assets.newamerica.net/blogposts/
   2012lifting_the_medicaid_asset_test_a_step_in_the_right_direction-66214.

7 Katherine Baicker et al., "The Oregon Experiment—Effects of Medicaid on
   Clinical Outcomes," *New England Journal of Medicine* 368, no. 18 (May 2, 2013):
   1713–22.

8 One estimate found that states that do not expand Medicaid will forego over
   $8 billion in federal funding and face $1 billion in greater state spending on
   uncompensated care in 2016. See Carter C. Price and Christine Eibner, "For
   States That Opt Out of Medicaid Expansion: 3.6 Million Fewer Insured and
   $8.4 Billion Less in Federal Payments," *Health Affairs* 32, no. 6 (June 2013):
   1030–36.

9 In July 2012, shortly after the Supreme Court ruling, the Congressional Budget Office estimated that in 2022, eight years after the implementation of
   the ACA, 30 million people would remain uninsured. See "Estimates for the
   Insurance Coverage Provisions of the Affordable Care Act for the Recent
   Supreme Court Decision," July 2012, http://www.cbo.gov/sites/default/files/
   cbofiles/attachments/43472-07-24-2012-CoverageEstimates.pdf. See also Robert Pear, "States' Policies on Health Care Exclude Poorest," *New York Times*,
   May 25, 2013.

10 Bruce Lesley, president of the child advocacy group First Focus, quoted in
   Pear, "States' Policies on Health Care Exclude Poorest."

11 Ricardo Alonso-Zaldivar, "Some Families to Be Priced Out of Health
   Overhaul," Associated Press, January 30, 2013, http://bigstory.ap.org/article/
   some-families-be-priced-out-health-overhaul.

12 Pamela Farley Short, Katherine Swartz, Namrata Uberoi, and Deborah R.
   Graefe, "Realizing Health Reform's Potential: Maintaining Coverage, Affordability, and Shared Responsibility When Income and Employment Change,"
   Commonwealth Fund, May 19, 2011, http://www.commonwealth fund.org/~/
   media/Files/Publications/Issue%20Brief/2011/May/1503_Short_maintaining
   _coverage_affordability_reform_brief.pdf.

13 Reed Abelson, "Choice of Health Plans to Vary Sharply from State to State,"
   New York Times, June 16, 2013.

14 Kaiser Family Foundation, "Rate Review: Spotlight on State Efforts to Make Health Insurance More Affordable," December 2010, http://kaiserfamily foundation.files.wordpress.com/2013/01/8122.pdf.

15 I used the "shop and compare tool" at https://www.coveredca.com/, January 11, 2014, and report the lowest monthly premium for each type of plan. At his income level, Dave would receive a subsidy on the monthly premiums (a tax credit), with the Enhanced Silver plan additionally subsidizing his out-of-pocket costs.

16 Institute of Medicine, *The Future of Disability in America* (Washington, DC: National Academies Press, 2007), 228.

17 See the conversation between Harold Pollack and disability law expert Sam Bagenstos, "Obamacare and the Disability Community," Healthinsurance.org Curbside Consult, June 19, 2013, http://www.healthinsurance.org/blog/2013/06/19/obamacares-promises-for-the-disability-community/, particularly the fifth section, "Medicaid Expansion and the Disabled."

18 Note that even if CLASS had been in place before Marcella's accident, it wouldn't have helped, because she hadn't worked long enough to be vested. The fiscal cliff legislation did set up a commission to study LTC issues, although Congress is not required to vote on its recommendations.

19 In the face of large premium increases, even those with private LTC coverage often end up reducing their coverage, such as decreasing the number of years of coverage, their daily benefit, or their inflation protection. The entire LTC insurance industry is in trouble, having set premiums too low during the 1980s and 1990s and underestimating how long seniors would be using the policies. Now it is contracting: only a dozen insurers are selling the policies, down from one hundred in the early 2000s. See Kelly Greene and Leslie Scism, "Long-Term-Care Insurance Gap Hits Seniors," *Wall Street Journal*, July 1, 2013, http://online.wsj.com/news/articles/SB10001424127887323475304578501820197828966.

20 Jacob S. Hacker, *The Road to Nowhere: The Genesis of President Clinton's Plan for Health Security* (Princeton, NJ: Princeton University Press, 1997) and *The Divided Welfare State: The Battle over Public and Private Social Benefits in the United States* (New York: Cambridge University Press, 2002); Theda Skocpol, *Boomerang: Clinton's Health Security Effort and the Turn against Government in U.S. Politics* (New York: W. W. Norton, 1996).

21 With the dual eligibles demonstration projects it authorizes, the ACA might even be perceived as a threat to the disabled. See the discussion of the Massachusetts duals demonstration in chapter 5. That said, Harold Pollack points

out (private communication) that some elements of the ACA may ultimately help the disabled. For example, the Balancing Incentive Program is aimed at states whose LTC expenses are weighted toward institutional care. It raises the matching rate that such states receive for home and community services if they commit to increasing access to such services.

22 David Gorn, "As Healthy Families Shift Goes, So Goes Rural Expansion of Medi-Cal Managed Care," *California Healthline*, November 7, 2013, http://www.californiahealthline.org/insight/2013/as-healthy-families-shift-goes-so-goes-rural-expansion-of-medical-managed-care. See also State of California Department of Health Care Services, "Medi-Cal Managed Care Rural Expansion," accessed February 28, 2014, http://www.dhcs.ca.gov/provgovpart/pages/mmcdruralexpansion.aspx. The managed care system is called Partnership HealthPlan of California.

23 The Shasta Community Health Center is a federally qualified health center, an organization that receives grants under the Public Health Service Act and enhanced reimbursement from Medicare and Medicaid to provide services to underserved areas or populations. US Department of Health and Human Services, "What Are Federally Qualified Health Centers (FQHCs)?," accessed February 28, 2014, http://www.hrsa.gov/healthit/toolbox/RuralHealthITtoolbox/Introduction/qualified.html.

24 Under the new managed care arrangement, Marcella also had to change several of her medicines because they weren't on the managed care program's drug formulary.

25 Federal Medicaid rules, updated most recently in the Deficit Reduction Act of 2005 (states may have different rules), allow the spouse in the community to keep the house, a car, and half the couple's joint "countable" assets up to a certain amount (which was $113,640 in 2012, a figure adjusted annually for inflation). There is also a five-year look-back period on asset transfers. Any assets transferred from the eventually disabled spouse to the community spouse during the five years before the disabled spouse enters a nursing home count against Medicaid eligibility in the following way: the amount of money transferred is divided by the average cost of a nursing home in one's state. The result of this computation gives the number of months the disabled spouse is ineligible for Medicaid. So if the disabled spouse had given away $60,000 in assets in a state where nursing homes cost $5,000 per month, he or she would be ineligible for Medicaid for twelve months. The 2005 DRA also changed the date when the penalty period begins. Previously, the twelve-month penalty period (in this example) started when the asset

transfer began. Now it begins after the person has moved to the nursing home, has spent down to the Medicaid asset limit, has applied for Medicaid, and has been approved except for the asset transfer. So if a person transferred $60,000 on January 1, 2010, moved to a nursing home on January 1, 2011, and spent down to Medicaid eligibility a few months later on May 1, 2011, the twelve-month penalty period would begin then, and Medicaid would not begin paying the person's nursing home bills until May 1, 2012. See http://www.elderlawanswers.com/medicaids-asset-transfer-rules-12015, accessed accessed February 28, 2014.

26 CWD is part of an initiative at the federal and state levels, such as the Ticket to Work program, whereby policy makers have tried to increase the incentives for the disabled to work without losing their health benefits or other assistance. See the US Social Security Administration, "2013 Red Book: A Guide to Work Incentives," http://www.ssa.gov/redbook/.

27 World Institute on Disability, Disability Benefits 101, "How Much Does California Working Disabled (CWD) Medi-Cal Cost?," accessed February 28, 2014, http://ca.db101.org/ca/programs/health_coverage/medi_cal/250/faqs .htm#_q725.

28 See World Institute on Disability, Disability Benefits 101, Medi-Cal: FAQs, "What Is the Medi-Cal California Working Disabled Program (CWD)?," accessed February 28, 2014, http://ca.db101.0rg/ca/programs/health_coverage/ medi_cal/250/faqs.htm#_q651.

29 The difference in countable income between Share of Cost Medi-Cal and CWD is this: Dave's income is included in the "countable income" calculation as part of Medi-Cal's "deeming rules" that add a spouse's income and assets to those of the disabled person; that's why the couple has to pay such a large Share of Cost. However, the CWD program does not count unearned income from private or public disability benefits. Thus, Marcella's SSI benefits are not included in their countable income. Also, the CWD program uses Social Security's countable income calculation to determine the disabled person's income, which excludes some earnings. See World Institute on Disability, Disability Benefits 101, Medi-Cal: The Details, "SSI-Linked Medi-Cal," http://ca.db101.0rg/ca/programs/health_coverage/medi_cal/program2a .htm#SSILinked.

30 State of California Department of Health Care Services, All County Welfare Directors Letter no. 11–38, November 9, 2011, http://www.dhcs.ca.gov/ services/medi-cal/eligibility/Documents/c11-38.pdf.

31 For "covered" disabled workers who are eligible for SSDI rather than SSI, a different set of work incentives applies. These provisions allow disabled peo-

ple to retain their SSDI and Medicare benefits while working. See US Social Security Administration, "Work Incentives: General Information," accessed February 28, 2014, http://www.ssa.gov/disabilityresearch/wi/generalinfo .htm#work. The trick is that by the time someone has gone through the arduous eligibility process and five-month waiting period for SSDI, and then made it through the even longer twenty-four-month Medicare waiting period, he or she may well be unemployable. See the conversation between Harold Pollack and disability law expert Sam Bagenstos, "Obamacare and the Disability Community."

32 The Medicare Modernization Act of 2003 added Part D to Medicare. Part D permits senior citizens to purchase prescription drug plans from private insurers (prescription drugs were not included in the Medicare program when it was passed in 1965). In order to bring the cost of the new benefit under a $410-billion-over-ten-years limit agreed upon by lawmakers, the standard drug benefit has a band of zero coverage. In 2013, for example, the standard plan paid 75 percent of drug costs below $2,970 in annual spending and 95 percent above $4,750, but paid nothing in between, leaving a coverage gap (the "doughnut") where individuals had to pay the entire cost of their drugs themselves. See Kimberly J. Morgan and Andrea Louise Campbell, *The Delegated Welfare State: Medicare, Markets, and the Governance of Social Policy* (New York: Oxford University Press, 2011). More controversially, the ACA cuts reimbursements to Medicare managed care plans (called Medicare Advantage), which had been raised to 114 percent of the cost of per-person traditional Medicare by the same 2003 legislation. See Kaiser Family Foundation, "Summary of New Health Reform Law," Publication no. 8061, April 25, 2011, http://www.kff.org/healthreform/upload/8061.pdf.

33 Robert B. Friedland, "The Coverage Puzzle: How the Pieces Fit Together," paper presented at the annual conference of the National Academy of Social Insurance, Washington, DC, January 24–25, 2002.

34 Pollack and Bagenstos, "Obamacare and the Disability Community," section 6, "The Lost Opportunity of the CLASS Act."

35 This section is based on Francesca Colombo et al., "Help Wanted? Providing and Paying for Long-Term Care" (Paris: OECD Health Policy Studies, Organisation for Economic Co-operation and Development, 2011), www .oecd.org/els/healthpoliciesanddata/47836116.pdf. In addition, see Robert Applebaum, Anthony Bardo, and Emily Robbins, "International Approaches to Long-Term Services and Supports," April 2, 2013, http://www.asaging .org/blog/international-approaches-long-term-services-and-supports; and Markus Kraus et al., "A Typology of Long-Term Care Systems in Europe"

(Brussels: ENEPRI Research Report no. 91 for the Assessing Needs of Care in European Nations [ANCIEN] research project, European Network of Economic Policy Research Institutes, 2010), http://www.ceps.be/book/typology -long-term-care-systems-europe.

36 Applebaum, Bardo, and Robbins, "International Approaches to Long-Term Services and Supports."

37 Pollack and Bagenstos, "Obamacare and the Disability Community," section 6, "The Lost Opportunity of the CLASS Act."

38 The LTC payroll tax is 0.25 percent higher for Germans without children. Colombo et al., "Help Wanted?"

39 Kimberly J. Morgan, "America's Misguided Approach to Social Welfare: How the Country Could Get More for Less," *Foreign Affairs* 92, no. 1 (January– February 2013): 153–64.

40 Julia Lynch, "A Cross-National Perspective on the American Welfare State," in *Oxford Handbook of Social Policy*, ed. Daniel Béland, Christopher Howard, and Kimberly Morgan (Oxford: Oxford University Press); this article now available online for downloading as of January 2014, accessed March 5, 2014, at http://www.oxfordhandbooks.com/view/10.1093/oxford hb/9780199838509.001.0001/oxfordhb-9780199838509-e-023.

41 On the treatment of welfare recipients in particular, see Joe Soss, Richard C. Fording, and Sanford F. Schram, *Disciplining the Poor: Neoliberal Paternalism and the Persistent Power of Race* (Chicago: University of Chicago Press, 2011).

42 Personal interview, May 17, 2013.

43 See also Julia Lynch, *Age in the Welfare State: The Origins of Social Spending on Pensioners, Workers, and Children* (New York: Cambridge University Press, 2006).

44 Jody Heymann, Alison Earle, and Jeffrey Hayes, "The Work, Family, and Equity Index: How Does the United States Measure Up?," Project on Global Working Families, McGill University Institute for Health and Social Policy, 2007, http://www.mcgill.ca/files/ihsp/WFEI2007.pdf. In 2010, Australia, the last industrialized country besides the United States without paid leave for new parents, passed a law guaranteeing eighteen weeks of such leave, at the federal minimum wage. See Jennifer Ludden, "US Only Industrialized Country with No Paid Leave for New Parents," June 17, 2010, National Public Radio, http://www.npr.org/blogs/thetwo-way/2010/06/17/127904924/u-s-now-only -industrialized-nation-without-paid-leave-for-new-parents.

45 US Department of Labor, "Fact Sheet #28: The Family and Medical Leave Act of 1993," revised February 2010, http://www.dol.gov/whd/fmla/; and Jane

Waldfogel, "Family and Medical Leave: Evidence from the 2000 Surveys," *Monthly Labor Review* 134, no. 9 (2001): 17–23.

46 Kimberly J. Morgan, "La conciliation travail/famille" (Policies for Work/Life Balance), *Informations Sociales*, no. 177 (May–June 2013): 60–71. Forty states offer public pre-K to 3- and 4-year-olds (mostly the latter). Including both general and special education enrollments, 31 percent of 4-year-olds and 7 percent of 3-year-olds are in public pre-K (with Head Start included, 41 percent of 4-year-olds and 14 percent of 3-year-olds are enrolled). However, the majority of states offering public pre-K have cut funding in recent years, and enrollment has stagnated. And as with other state-run programs, variation is huge. The proportion of children enrolled in state pre-kindergarten in 2011–12 ranged from 79 percent in Florida to 0.9 percent in Rhode Island; in the median state, 21 percent were enrolled. See W. Steven Barnett, Megan E. Carolan, Jen Fitzgerald, and James H. Squires, *The State of Preschool 2012: State Preschool Yearbook* (New Brunswick, NJ: National Institute for Early Education Research, 2012).

47 Morgan, "La conciliation travail/famille." The Dependent Care Assistance Program—known more familiarly as flexible spending plans—essentially allows employees to use up to $5,000 in pretax dollars to pay for child care. As with many other tax expenditure programs, the higher one's income, the more this tax break is worth. Under the Dependent Care Tax Credit, families can deduct up to 35 percent of child care costs for a maximum of $3,000 for one child and $6,000 for two or more. The deduction phases out as income rises, however, such that only those making $15,000 can actually deduct 35 percent of their costs—but such families probably have very little income tax to begin with, and the deduction isn't worth much to higher-income families (the average claim in 2009 was only $528). Two other tax breaks— the Child Tax Credit and EITC—can be used to cover child care costs, and benefit more low-income people because they are "refundable": that is, the credit can be larger than the tax liability, resulting in a net payment. However, these tax credits pale in comparison with the full cost of day care, particularly in metropolitan areas, where it can reach $15,000 per year or more.

48 The federal Child Care Development Block Grant provides states with funds to provide child care vouchers, but in 2010 just 1.7 million children of the 7.7 million eligible received CCDBG funding. Head Start too funds child care for low-income children, but covered just over 1 million children in 2010, fewer than half of those eligible. Morgan, "La conciliation travail/famille." See also Heather Hahn, Olivia Golden, and Peter Edelman, "Strengthening

TANF for States and Needy Families," Urban Institute, August 22, 2012, http:// www.urban.org/UploadedPDF/412636-Strengthening-TANF-for-States-and -Needy-Families.pdf.

Another concern in the United States is day care quality. Only 10 percent of day care operations provide high-quality care as measured by "regulable features" such as adult-to-child ratio, group size, and caregivers' education levels, and by "process features" of "positive caregiving"—"sensitive, encouraging, and frequent interactions between the caregiver and the child." National Institute of Child Health Development, "The NICHD Study of Early Child Care and Youth Development," US Department of Health and Human Services, January 2006, https://www.nichd.nih.gov/research/supported/Pages/ seccyd.aspx. Also see Jonathan Cohn, "The Hell of American Day Care," *The New Republic*, April 15, 2013, 22–27.

49 Janet C. Gornick and Marcia K. Meyers, *Families That Work: Policies for Reconciling Parenthood and Employment* (New York: Russell Sage Foundation, 2003). Some scholars assert that women in high-level occupations face less discrimination in countries having fewer work-family policies, such as the United States (see Hadas Mandel and Moshe Semyonov, "A Welfare State Paradox: State Interventions and Women's Employment Opportunities in 22 Countries," *American Journal of Sociology* 111 [May 2006]: 1910–49). However, if such effects exist, they are in countries on the extreme end of the parental leave continuum (more than a year).

50 US Department of Labor, "Women in the Labor Force: A Databook," December 2011, table 7, http://www.bls.gov/cps/wlf-databook2011.htm.

51 Gornick and Meyers, *Families That Work*, 62.

52 Ibid.

53 Ibid., 1.

54 The New Jersey plan is similar (six weeks' paid leave for bonding or care funded by an employee payroll tax, with a weekly benefit rate at two-thirds of average weekly wages, for a maximum of $572). New Jersey Department of Labor and Workforce Development, "Family Leave Insurance Benefits— General Information," accessed February 28, 2014, http://lwd.dol.state.nj.us/ labor/fli/content/program_info_menu.html.

55 Eileen Appelbaum and Ruth Milkman, "Paid Family Leave Pays Off in California," Harvard Business Review HBR Blog Network/Research, January 19, 2011, http://blogs.hbr.org/research/2011/01/paid-family-leave-pays-off-in.html. Also, Ruth Milkman and Eileen Appelbaum, *Unfinished Business: Paid Family Leave in California and the Future of U.S. Work-Family Policy* (Ithaca, NY: Cornell University Press, 2013).

56 This point is implicit in Julia Lynch's article, "A Cross-National Perspective on the American Welfare State," and the statistics cited in this paragraph are from that piece.

57 Paul Sullivan, "Planning for Retirement? Don't Forget Health Care Costs," *New York Times*, October 6, 2012. Entities such as the Employment Benefit Research Institute calculate similar amounts.

58 Employment Benefit Research Institute, Retirement Confidence Survey, "Age Comparisons among Workers," 2012 RCS Fact Sheet #4, http://www.ebri.org/pdf/surveys/rcs/2012/fs-04-rcs-12-fs4-age.pdf.

59 The United States is compared with sixteen European nations. See Luxembourg Income Study data as cited in Alfred Stepan and Juan J. Linz, "Comparative Perspectives on Inequality and the Quality of Democracy in the United States," *Perspectives on Politics* 9, no. 4 (December 2011): 941–56. At least health outcomes among older Americans resemble those of older residents in other rich democracies (unlike the health outcomes of working-aged Americans, which are far worse because so many lack insurance). See Karen Davis, Cathy Schoen, and Kristof Stremikis, "Mirror, Mirror on the Wall: How the Performance of the U.S. Health Care System Compares Internationally," 2010 update, Commonwealth Fund, June 2010, http://www.commonwealthfund.org/~/media/Files/Publications/Fund%20Report/2010/Jun/1400_Davis_Mirror_Mirror_on_the_wall_2010.pdf.

60 The statistics cited here are for TANF monthly benefits in New Hampshire and Mississippi. I used the Economic Policy Institute's Family Budget Calculator to calculate the cost-of-living difference. The calculator "measures the income a family needs in order to attain a secure yet modest living standard by estimating community-specific costs of housing, food, child care, transportation, health care, other necessities, and taxes" for 615 US communities in 2013. See http://www.epi.org/resources/budget/, accessed February 28, 2014. For a one-adult, two-child household, the family budgets for the largest cities in New Hampshire and Mississippi are $66,317 and $48,556, respectively, while the budgets for each state's rural areas are $67,157 and $45,028, for ratios of 1.4 and 1.5 to 1.

61 Many thanks to Kimberly Morgan for these points.

62 The United States is included in a study of seventeen advanced-economy nations. See Institute of Medicine, "U.S. Health in International Perspective: Shorter Lives, Poorer Health," January 2013, http://www.iom.edu/Reports/2013/US-Health-in-International-Perspective-Shorter-Lives-Poorer-Health.aspx.

63 Commonwealth Fund, "Why Not the Best? Results from the National Score-

card on U.S. Health System Performance, 2011," October 2011, http://www
.commonwealthfund.org/Publications/Fund-Reports/2011/Oct/Why-Not
-the-Best-2011.aspx?page=all.

64 Howard Steven Friedman, *The Measure of a Nation* (Amherst, NY: Prometheus
Books, 2012).

65 Timothy M. Smeeding, Robert Erikson, and Markus Jantti, eds., *Persistence,
Privilege, and Parenting: The Comparative Study of Intergenerational Mobility*
(New York: Russell Sage Foundation, 2011); Miles Corak, "Income Inequality, Equality of Opportunity, and Intergenerational Mobility," *Journal of Economic Perspectives* 27, no. 3 (Summer 2013): 79–102.

66 Friedman, *The Measure of a Nation*; Commonwealth Fund, "Why Not the
Best?"

67 Under Social Security private account proposals, a portion of the payroll tax
would be diverted from the traditional program into accounts that individuals would manage, selecting from a menu of investment options in stocks or
bonds. The size of the individual accounts at retirement would depend on
the choice of investment vehicles and the performance of the equity markets; thus, such a reform reduces the defined benefit (traditional) portion of
Social Security and introduces a new defined contribution portion, the value
of which in retirement is unknown. Medicare premium support or voucher
proposals have several different structures, but the basic idea is to convert
Medicare from the traditional program, in which the government reim-
burses senior citizens' medical bills on an open-ended basis, into a program
in which seniors would receive a voucher to purchase a private insurance
plan. They would have to pay the difference if their selected plan costs more
than the value of the voucher. Such a reform would cap the government's
spending.

68 The budget plans advocated by Representative Paul Ryan (R-Wisc.) proposed
particularly deep cuts in social assistance (see his Roadmap for America's
Future, accessed February 28, 2014, http://roadmap.republicans.budget
.house.gov/), but Medicaid and domestic discretionary spending were
trimmed quite a bit even in the recommendations of the more moderate
Bowles-Simpson National Commission on Fiscal Responsibility and Reform
and Domenici-Rivlin Debt Reduction Task Force, both of 2010.

69 Megan Woolhouse, "Federal Cuts Hitting Housing Subsidy Program," *Boston Globe*, May 26, 2013, http://www.bostonglobe.com/business/2013/05/25/
federal-cuts-hit-housing-programs-for-poor/9Su1qvU95EMoKf2uvt5HCL/
story.html.

70 Akilah Johnson, "Spending Cuts Taking Hard Toll on Head Start," *Boston*

Globe, June 10, 2013, http://www.bostonglobe.com/metro/2013/06/09/head-start-lose-more-seats-than-expected-legacy-from-sequestration/RUI6rjrJlvp MnUaJRrTi6M/story.html.

71 Paul Fronstin, "Sources of Health Insurance and Characteristics of the Uninsured: Analysis of the March 2012 Current Population Survey," Employee Benefit Research Institute Policy Brief no. 376, September 2012, http://www.ebri.org/publications/ib/index.cfm?fa=ibDisp&content_id=5114.

72 Congressional Budget Office, "Growth in Means-Tested Programs and Tax Credits for Low-Income Households," February 2013, http://www.cbo.gov/sites/default/files/cbofiles/attachments/43934-Means-TestedPrograms.pdf, p. 20.

73 Followed by foundations (which gave 14 percent of total), bequests (8 percent), and corporations (5 percent). National Philanthropic Trust, "Charitable Giving Statistics," accessed February 28, 2014, http://www.nptrust.org/philanthropic-resources/charitable-giving-statistics.

74 Organisation for Economic Co-operation and Development, OECD Revenue Statistics—Comparative Tables, http://stats.oecd.org/Index.aspx?QueryId =21699, December 2, 2013.

75 Peter Lindert, *Growing Public: Social Spending and Economic Growth since the Eighteenth Century* (Cambridge: Cambridge University Press, 2004); Joel Slemrod and Jon Bakija, *Taxing Ourselves: A Citizen's Guide to the Debate over Taxes*, 4th ed. (Cambridge, MA: MIT Press, 2008).

76 Harold Pollack, "We Are All Vulnerable: Medicaid, Health Reform, and the 2012 Election," accessed February 28, 2014, http://www.youtube.com/watch ?v=Z4-EGUif_N0&feature=player_embedded.

GLOSSARY

Access for Infants and Mothers (AIM): The state of California's health insurance plan for middle-income pregnant women.

Affordable Care Act (ACA): The Obama administration health reform formally known as the Patient Protection and Affordable Care Act of 2010. This national legislation reformed the American health insurance system by requiring individuals to have health insurance, expanding **Medicaid** (later made optional for states by the Supreme Court), requiring employers above a certain size to offer health insurance, and creating insurance marketplaces where individuals without employer-provided coverage can purchase health insurance. It also established new regulations for private insurers.

Aid to Families with Dependent Children (AFDC). See **TANF.**

California Working Disabled Program (CWD): A California program that encourages the disabled to work without interfering with Medi-Cal eligibility by allowing working disabled enrollees to buy into Medi-Cal through a sliding-scale monthly premium payment.

Centers for Independent Living (CILs): Nonprofit organizations run by and for people with disabilities. CILs are nonresidential facilities that assist the disabled with daily living issues. They provide housing information, peer counseling, personal assistant services, independent living skills training, legal aid, assistive technology services, employment readiness training, benefits counseling, and referrals.

Child Care Development Block Grant (CCDBG): A federal block grant that provides states with the funding for child care vouchers for low-income children.

Child Tax Credit: A federal tax credit intended to subsidize the cost of raising children for low- and middle-income families.

Children's Health Insurance Program (CHIP): A federal-state program that provides health insurance to lower-income children. Eligibility criteria vary by state.

Community Living Assistance Services and Supports (CLASS): A voluntary **social insurance** program for **long-term care** originally contained in the **Affordable Care Act.** Workers could pay into the system and would be eligible for a daily long-term care allowance with no lifetime limit. The program was repealed in 2012, because it was deemed fiscally unsustainable.

Consolidated Omnibus Budget Reconciliation Act (COBRA): A health benefit provision that allows those who have lost their job to continue to buy into their employer's health insurance plan for up to eighteen months at the group rate, which is typically far less than the costs of health insurance on the individual market.

Dependent Care Assistance Program: A flexible spending plan that allows employees of participating employers to use up to $5,000 in pretax income to pay for child care.

Dependent Care Tax Credit: A federal tax credit under which families can deduct a proportion of child care costs. The deduction phases out as income rises.

Earned Income Tax Credit (EITC): A federal tax credit targeted at low-wage workers that refunds part or all of the federal income and payroll taxes they pay. Some states have a state version in addition.

Family and Medical Leave Act (FMLA): National legislation passed in 1993 that allows eligible employees to take up to twelve weeks of unpaid leave during any twelve-month period in case of illness, to care for a family member, or to care for a newborn or newly adopted child.

food stamps. See **Supplemental Nutrition Assistance Program.**

General Assistance or General Relief: State-level programs providing cash assistance to low-income adults without dependents. Many states have severely reduced or eliminated such programs. Eligibility criteria and availability vary by state and sometimes by county or city.

Head Start: A federal program that funds child care for low-income children as well as other family health, nutrition, and social services.

In-Home Support Services (IHSS): A California program that pays for home-based personal care assistance for Medi-Cal recipients.

long-term services and supports (LTSS)/long-term care (LTC): *Long-term services and supports* refers to the services needed by the disabled community, including supports to help the disabled live independently at home. *Long-term care* more typically refers to medicalized care for the disabled, particularly the elderly.

Low-Income Home Energy Assistance Program (LIHEAP): A federal heating assistance program for low-income people.

Medicaid/Medi-Cal: Medicaid is a joint federal-state program providing public health insurance for the poor, enacted in 1965. Medi-Cal is California's version of Medicaid. Above minimum federal guidelines, eligibility varies by state.

Medicare: A federally run public health insurance program for older Americans, enacted in 1965. Eligibility and benefits are uniform nationwide.

medigap supplemental insurance: Supplemental health plans that individuals on **Medicare** over the age of sixty-five can purchase from private insurers to help cover out-of-pocket costs, such as Medicare coinsurance and deductibles. Disabled persons under sixty-five on Medicare are not allowed to buy medigap plans.

Section 8 housing vouchers: A federal program that provides subsidized housing vouchers for low-income households renting private-market apartments.

Share of Cost Medi-Cal (SOC Medi-Cal): A version of Medi-Cal in which beneficiaries incur a certain amount of health care expenses each month before **Medi-Cal** coverage commences. When the individual or family has met the share of cost, Medi-Cal pays for any additional covered expenses for the month. It is akin to having a high-deductible catastrophic insurance plan for which the deductible resets every month.

social assistance: The set of American means-tested social programs intended for the poor, such as **Medicaid, TANF,** and food stamps/**SNAP**. Social assistance programs are typically funded by general tax revenues, and target low-income groups.

social insurance: The set of "universal" social programs, such as **Social Security** and **Medicare,** for which all qualified workers are eligible. It is funded at least in part by earmarked taxes or "contributions" imposed on workers and/or employers.

Social Security Disability Insurance (SSDI): A program established within **Social Security** in 1956 that provides a monthly cash benefit to the permanently disabled. It is funded by a payroll tax on workers.

Social Security retirement benefits: A federal program established in 1935 that provides a monthly cash benefit to retired older individuals. It is funded by a payroll tax on workers.

Social Security survivors benefits: A federal program within **Social Security** that provides a monthly cash benefit to the surviving spouse and minor children of deceased workers. It is funded by a payroll tax on workers.

Supplemental Nutrition Assistance Program (SNAP): The federal "food stamp" program providing a monthly food assistance benefit to low-income individuals and families.

Supplemental Security Income (SSI): A federal program providing cash assistance to poor elderly, blind, and disabled people.

take-up rate: The proportion of people eligible for a program who actually enroll.

tax expenditures: The formal name for tax breaks in the form of exemptions, deductions, or credits to certain groups or for specific activities. Social-purpose tax expenditures are one type, by which the government provides social benefits not through direct expenditures but by foregoing revenue. Examples include the **Earned Income Tax Credit**, the home mortgage interest deduction, and the tax break for employer-provided health insurance and retirement plans.

Temporary Assistance for Needy Families (TANF): A federal-state program that provides cash assistance to low-income families with children. Eligibility criteria vary by state.

Unemployment Insurance (UI): A **social insurance** program that provides time-limited cash assistance for workers who have been laid off. It is funded by state and federal payroll taxes on employers, but states set the eligibility criteria.

Welfare. See **TANF.**

Women, Infants and Children (WIC): A supplemental nutritional program for lower-income pregnant and breast-feeding women, infants, and children under the age of five at nutritional risk. The federal government sets income eligibility guidelines and provides grants to states.

workers' compensation: A mostly state-run **social insurance** program providing benefits to injured workers.

INDEX